ISBN: 978129036650

Published by:
HardPress Publishing
8345 NW 66TH ST #2561
MIAMI FL 33166-2626

Email: info@hardpress.net
Web: http://www.hardpress.net

4,50

Jno E. Frost

& others $1.00

" ' LET THEM OPPOSE,' HE SAID, STURDILY "

The Sixth Sense

and Other Stories

By

MARGARET SUTTON BRISCOE

Author of "Jimty, and Others"

Illustrated

NEW YORK AND LONDON

HARPER & BROTHERS PUBLISHERS

1899

TO

THE HON. HENRY E. HOWLAND

In Memory of

"PROVINCIA"

To the editors of *Harper's Periodicals*, *The Century Magazine*, and *Scribner's Magazine*, I wish to express my thanks for the privilege of reprinting the stories collected in this volume.

M. S. B.

CONTENTS

ILLUSTRATIONS

THE SIXTH SENSE

"Don't take it so, Helen. You were pre-pared for this, my dear; it might be so much worse."

"Worse! Oh, mother, this is the worst!"

"Oh, no, no, dear—no! You aren't a mother yourself, or you'd feel at once what I mean. The last six months of doubts nearly maddened me. Now that we know he is dead, it is we only who suffer; but alive—he might be enduring everything."

Helen shuddered rebelliously, lifting her head from her mother's knee and wiping away her tears.

"Mamma, I can't look at things the way you do. You only allow a choice between Jack horribly maimed or dead. I can't think of him as anything but alive and well, and so strong and big, and loving us so."

"Don't, don't, dear!" cried the mother, sharp-ly. She broke into sudden, violent weeping. "I can't stand this. Let me bear it my own way."

A   I

The two women clung together again, the ruthless young lips that had beaten down the mother's hard-won philosophy showering repentant kisses.

"Do you think," Helen whispered, softly, "that it would hurt you too much to tell me a little more now?"

"I should like to," said Mrs. Duain, simply. "It always helps me, to talk things over. The young fellow was very kind. He said he would have come to see us before, but he was wounded himself at Gettysburg—not an hour after he left our boy dead on the field—and ill in hospital for a long time. And then he didn't know we had no news of Jack. It was the merest chance goodness of heart, a kindness for a dead comrade, that made him come to us. He thought we might like to know what Jack's last words were. He saw the last breath leave his lips; his knee was under Jack's head as he passed away, just as mine is under yours, Helen."

"Oh, mamma!" groaned the girl, protesting involuntarily.

"I won't tell you more if it distresses you, dear. I preferred to hear all myself, though I felt it impossible to bear at first, just as you do."

"Don't tell me any more, mamma — later perhaps. But just one thing—what were his last words?"

"Of us, dear : 'Mother—Helen—my love.' That was what his comrade came to bring us."

The mother's lips quivered as she gave the message, but she would not give way. Helen sobbed uncontrollably.

"Oh, Jack! Dear, dearest Jack! To remember me too—to send us his love—"

Mrs. Duain laid her hand comfortingly on the bowed head.

"I have something more to tell you, something that ought to comfort you. It has me," she said, softly. "Those last words were not all for you and me. They seemed to be only a message to us ; even his messenger thought they were ; but it was not just your name and mine and his love to us that Jack meant, Helen. Those last two words, 'My Love,' were not as a message to us at all, but as a *name* to him. He has left us a legacy."

Helen sat upright on the floor at her mother's feet, pushing back the hair from her wet face and looking up in wonder.

"Something very extraordinary and very beautiful has happened. I have lost a son and gained a daughter in the same hour. Did you know that Jack was engaged to be married?"

Helen did not reply in words. Motionless listening answered for her ignorance.

"It's quite true, dear; she has just told me herself. She came in to call formally—a formal call from her seems strange to think of now; she was shown into this room just as Jack's comrade left me. I was utterly overcome. You were away, and I needed some one. Poor child! she was needing care herself. And there was I, blind thing, crying and sobbing and blurting out the news of my loss to her. I might have gone on forever if I hadn't heard something in her voice that made me look up suddenly, and then I saw her poor face; but the voice was enough. Do you remember the story of the old friend who wrote to a widow when her husband died just two words—'Oh, Madam!' That story always touched me so. All this poor child said was, 'Oh, Mrs. Duain!' and it was like a tortured cry."

Helen caught her mother's hands eagerly—so much hung on a word, a name.

"But, mamma, you haven't told me—you haven't once said—"

"Hush!" whispered Mrs. Duain, quickly; "here she is. Did you suppose I could part

4

with her at once? Don't let her know that I have told you, Helen. It is important, remember."

She had as well spoken warningly to the shifting winds. Every line of her daughter's expressive face was always as speakingly telltale as the mother's. As she now turned with intense eagerness towards the opening door, the woman who appeared on the threshold had only to give one glance at her before she paused, shrinking into the sheltering curtain and crying out, in a breathless reproach,

"Oh, Mrs. Duain, you said you would tell no one !"

Mrs. Duain hurried forward, but not so quickly as Helen. The young girl, with charming impulsiveness, sprang to the doorway and twined her arms about the reluctant figure thus hovering as it were on the outskirts of their family life. She drew her into the room with a large and generous motion of her strong young arms, that seemed to say this was but a symbol of what her heart was doing.

"Mamma couldn't help telling me. Wouldn't it have been cruel not to tell me? I shall love you so dearly. And you will love me, won't you, An—Annita?" She stumbled a little over the name, and laughed, half embarrassed, half

tearful. " That's your name, isn't it ? It seems
absurd that I shouldn't be quite sure, but, you
see, I haven't known you so very well—though
I always liked you ; and now shall you be able
to love me ?"

Annita Andrews—for that was her name—
looked silently and wistfully from one to the
other, her eyes lingering last on the eager
young face pressing near hers. In appearance
she was as unlike the mother and daughter,
with their clever, irregular features and vivid
faces, as it was possible to be. There could
never have been a woman born into the Duain
family with so delicately regular or so sealed a
face. Beauty of feature and a certain charm
of contrasting coloring she had, for the brown
eyes were clear and soft, the contour of the
face was beautiful and finely cut, the brow under the fair hair was shapely and low ; but,
with so much said, there was still to be ardently
desired something that was missing. The face
was uninteresting, lacking wholly change and
charm of expression. There was no proof of
that delightful perceptiveness and receptive-
ness which can render the plainest face womanly and attractive. An occasional wistfulness
in the too shallow brown of the eyes, a slightly
appealing droop of the mouth, were the only

claims to expression made by features that might have been extremely lovely if but a little less sealed. This was the woman who was vainly striving to reply to Helen Duain's impetuous approach, vainly seeking a voice which it seemed she could not force to obey her. Twice she tried to answer, but her words died away as they came ; and at last, with a glance of appealing reproach towards Mrs. Duain, she turned aside, burying her face in her hands.

"You have frightened her, dear. Give her to me," said Mrs. Duain, compassionately ; but Helen, with a stir at her breast, thought she felt the girl she still held in her arms move towards her, though ever so slightly, and drew her closer possessively. To take one to her, Mrs. Duain had to take both ; but of this her motherly arms were capable.

"I'm a hopelessly leaky old woman, my dear," she said. "You must try to forgive me, Annita. But, you see, Helen came in *just* after you had told me, and it seemed as if I had to tell her. If you hadn't *just* told me—"

She broke off with the implication that under other circumstances she would surely have guarded the secret jealously, which she doubtless believed, but none the less it was far from the truth, for Mrs. Duain was quite right when

7

she described herself as hopelessly leaky. Her sympathy was too sweet and real to lose at any price, so her friends went on confiding in her, even though knowing in the very moments of confidence that the price must be betrayal at some date, late or early, and a betrayal so naïve and inevitable that no one could complain very bitterly. Nor did Annita complain now, beyond that first reproachful glance.

"My two daughters !" said Mrs. Duain, with feeling, drawing the two heads down, one on either shoulder.

"Of course I love you, because you're a part of Jack," whispered Helen, across her mother's bosom. "If only Jack could see us now !"

"He does !" cried Mrs. Duain, fervently, glancing up ; "he does !"

Quick tears fell from her lashes down on the face of the girl she held so closely for that son's sake ; and as they fell, Annita looked up with a struggling, gasping breath. She spoke as if with an agony of effort.

"I—I can't stand this. I—"

"What are we thinking of ?" cried Mrs. Duain. "Of course this is too much for her." With her usual quickness of motion she thrust Helen from her and passed her hand over the

8

new daughter's quivering features, closing down the eyelids soothingly. "Rest there, my dear child. Stop thinking for a moment. No, don't try to talk." She stopped the quivering lips with her soft, motherly touch. The girl's face lay heavily on her shoulder. "Helen," cried Mrs. Duain, suddenly, "come quickly; she has fainted. Help me to the couch. Oh, poor, poor child!"

If Annita Andrews had been capable of thinking out a deliberate plan by which to steal her way most quickly into the hearts of Jack Duain's mother and sister, she could have fallen on no more subtle and instant method than this very real illness. It seemed at once to differentiate her grief from theirs, and set it apart as something more peculiarly sacred. Mrs. Duain knew that she still had one child, and Helen that she still had her mother; but both knew that Annita Andrews had nothing more of a home and family life than a room in an aunt's house—a home already complete in family and interests long before her entrance. In a vague, motherly way Mrs. Duain had often pitied the shy, undemonstrative girl, though that pity had never gone so far as to reach the point of interest. Annita Andrews had always seemed to her to lack place and background as a personal inheritance, and had never been able to conquer these for herself. Something of all this Mrs. Duain murmured in pitying accents to Helen across the unconscious figure, and Helen was thinking it all over as she sat by the side of the couch, gently chafing Annita's hands, and applying such home remedies as her mother's experience supplied. When the physician they had summoned came hurrying in he made no change in the treatment, pronouncing the attack harmless. It was, in fact, already beginning to yield. It seemed to Helen that she could see the swoon breaking under their efforts as still water breaks when a stone is flung into it. Signs of consciousness formed and broke and formed again in the white face, always in wider and wider circles. Now the eyelids quivered, and again the lips moved.

"Had she a fall?" the physician asked. He was an old family friend as well. "Did she have a fall or a blow?"

And Mrs. Duain assented : "A very heavy blow. My dear friend, we have just heard with certainty of my boy's death."

The physician forgot his patient and looked up quickly. "At last ! And what we all feared. Any news is better than none, dear madam, believe me. So he is really gone, and only last night we were talking of him."

"Where?" asked Mrs. Duain, with that eagerness for hearing praise of the dead which belongs to all who have lost by death—as our one poor hope of their earthly immortality. The old friend understood and humored the mother's wish.

"At a little dinner party. I wish you could have been there, only no ladies were present. Some one chanced to speak your boy's name, and there was instant silence. Then some one else said, out loud, 'How that man is remembered!' I sat next our host. I could see the water rise in his eyes as he got to his feet. '*Jack Duain*,' was all he said. We rose up to drink without another word. Nobody wanted to speak. That's the man he was. A son to miss indeed; a friend to lament. Do you mean me to understand that my patient here—" He paused.

"Yes," said Mrs. Duain, choking and wiping her eyes. "Oh yes, poor child. If he had lived she would have been his wife."

"Poor child indeed!" said the physician, with more than professional pity.

"Be quiet," cried Helen; "she hears us. I think she has heard you both all the time."

She had seen the last confining circle breaking. The color was rising in Annita's face; she opened her eyes and looked up at them. The physician approached gently, but his patient turned away sharply from his pitying gaze and again closed her eyes. He respected her implied wish.

"Her pulse is stronger," he said to Mrs. Duain. "She will do very well now, only I should advise entire quiet for a week at least. There has been a severe shock. I wish her aunt's house were a little less gay, a little less full of young people. Hers is anything but a quiet home."

"How much quieter could ours be!" said Mrs. Duain, quickly—"only Helen and me, and our house now one of mourning."

"Ah!" said the physician, bowing himself out from the room and from this story; "I understand. She is safer with you than with me, I see. You are still a good mother to your son, my dear Mrs. Duain."

Mrs. Duain sat down by the other side of the couch from Helen. "You heard, my dear," she said, quietly; "will you stay with us for a time and let us care for you?"

Annita looked up at her with a dazed expression. She struggled to sit up on the couch.

"Let you care for me?" she repeated. "Oh yes, yes; but I can't stay here. I can't stay here."

Both words and manner were feverishly distressed.

"Why not?" said Mrs. Duain, soothingly. "Now, my child, be reasonable. You are ill, but not too ill for me to talk a little plain sense to you. You know, we all know, that your aunt's house is not exactly a home to you. Indeed, it is not a home to any of them. They have never seemed to me to pause long enough to know each other — to love each other and show it. Why, caresses are as natural to Helen and me as breathing and living. Oh yes, I know they are all kind to you, but — is it like this?" And she stooped and gathered the girl into her arms.

"Don't refuse us," pleaded Helen, on the other side. "Don't, dear Annita. Pray, pray stay with us."

"Let us say only for this one week, then," urged Mrs. Duain, quick to yield part where she saw it wise.

Annita, her head languidly resting on Mrs. Duain's motherly shoulder, looked still, as if dazzled, from one eloquent face to the other, each saying quite as much in silence as when their lips spoke.

"I never saw love like this before," she faltered. Her lips quivered, her face flushed, and her eyes and mouth grew as self-pitiful as a lost child's. Mrs. Duain thought she had never seen her so near great beauty.

"I can only just remember my parents," the girl went on, brokenly, "and then came boarding-school, and then my aunt's home, and— yes, they are kind there, but it's not like this. No, I never saw love like this."

"Except from Jack," corrected Helen.

The crimson shot up over the white face in a blush so painful that Mrs. Duain, startled by the change, laid her finger on her lips, glancing silencingly at Helen. But in her heart she was exulting in the sight of a love that held its privacy so sacred. Death seemed less a separation when a girl's cheek blushed hotly for him who was gone from them forever. With a quick, womanly motion she stooped and hid the flushed face against her own protectingly. She could feel that Annita lay more and more closely in her warm embrace ; her hand was timidly returning the clasp of Helen's hand. Suddenly she lifted her head strongly and withdrew from them both ; but it was only to hold out her hands anew, with a motion as if offering herself freely to each of them. There was so little of native impulsiveness about her that the gesture carried more meaning than from another less reserved and shy.

"You will stay!" cried Helen, joyfully.

"I must," she answered. "I can't—no, I can't turn away love like this. I must take it, if only for this week." She paused to steady her voice. When she spoke again the effort made it seem almost hard. "Only for this week," she repeated, firmly.

It was rather an anxious week they spent together, as it could hardly fail to be with the conditions given. In the first place, little complications began at once to arise that ought to have been readily foretold, but that were evidently unforeseen by Annita, whose shrinking wish to keep her secret was the cause of trouble. The mere fact of her presence in the house at this time was, as Mrs. Duain well knew it must be, fair ground for comment; and there, too, were the girl's relations to be considered. After due thought, Mrs. Duain, who had her own rather imperial methods of adjusting affairs, made up her mind as to her course of action, and Annita's as well. The engagement was to be announced, not formally, but by a word spoken here and there. She meant to take no action without Annita's permission, but that permission she intended to have.

Annita Andrews, and indeed all of her family, though with as desirable a social standing as her own, had never interested Mrs. Duain particularly, and therefore they had never been allowed to know her except as an impersonal and delightful acquaintance. She knew now with shrewd intuition that through her circle of personal friends, Annita Andrews would learn to know her far better and more rapidly than by the most intimate personal relations. For this reason, among others, she would not wholly close her home as one of mourning. Outside, with its folded shutters and storm-doors bowed, the house wore that strangely human look of sad dignity which belongs to a closed home when death has touched the lintel ; but within life went on almost as it had before the coming of definite news of loss. It had been a house of doubt and semi-mourning for months. Now it was only certainty of grief. Friends came and went, bringing their messages of affection and sympathy, and all were received by Mrs. Duain, and to all she presented Annita Andrews with a quiet dignity which forbade questions, and yet with so careful recognition of her place as a member of the family that her manner could not fail to make its due impression. Very evidently what the girl herself longed for was to be let alone and allowed to look on in silence at this revealed family life, full of love and real friendships—plainly very different from anything to which she was accustomed. She tried always to sit a little apart, rather pale and with puzzled eyes, looking out from over her clasped hands, which she constantly held against her face, hiding lips that seemed to Helen's pitying eyes to be always quivering slightly. But this remoteness and silence was what Mrs. Duain would not allow. No one could have doubted her adoration of her son, but an unwholesome mourning in her house by herself or any one else was what she would not tolerate. She talked of her son constantly and to every one, as often with laughter as with tears ; for there was much in Jack Duain's short and merry life to recall with laughter. Helen expostulated with her mother in vain. To the younger woman there was a species of cruelty in the constant rousing of Annita from her dazed and dream-like condition, in the forcing her to meet new friends at this time. But Mrs. Duain had decided otherwise.

"We must rouse her," she insisted. "Don't

you see this is our chance to reach her now, while she is stirred? It's just as important for us to know her as for her to know us; and do you know her at all? I don't, yet half our week has gone. Hers is a very sealed nature. No, you must let me follow my own instinct."

But despite her theories, Mrs. Duain began to yield to an uncomfortable wonder if they ever could know Annita Andrews much better. She knew that some women were born to blow open wide as roses—she herself was one of these—while others were born to live tightly closed as button-flowers, and with the latter she began to classify Annita Andrews. There was something baffling, something inexpressibly trying, to her in the very docility and gentleness of this intimate yet stranger guest. Even the meeting - ground of a common grief had been practically closed from the first, for each effort to draw Annita to speech concerning her lover caused such evident suffering that Mrs. Duain had not the heart to persist too far in that direction. Yet something, she felt, must be done, for the girl's shyness and silence seemed to be increasing rather than decreasing, and the week of her promised stay was passing. It was then that the elder woman decided on a serious step, and only waited

18

for the best opportunity to take it safely. That chance seemed to her to open most fairly on the night when the mourning-bonnets came home—those last details of costume. On that evening Mrs. Duain, more full of thought than she showed, walked up the stairs to bed, a veil-draped bonnet in either hand, and another on her head. Having no free hand with which to hold her skirts away from her feet, she walked up the stairs with extreme difficulty, escaping her petticoats only by stepping in a pigeon-toed way, as do all women caught in like case. She was laughing like a girl at her own awkwardness, but seemed to be enjoying the exercise, for she refused aid, and at the upper landing turned to look smilingly down on the two girls following her.

" I did it," she said, merrily. " And look up at me, girls ! Isn't this Madame Milliner going to bed ?"

Helen, her hand still on the balustrade, stopped, and laughing naturally, looked up at the black - draped figure ; but the mother glanced beyond her and keenly at Annita. As the light from the high hall lamp fell full upon the girl's upraised face, Mrs. Duain thought she found there a fresher look and a less forced smile than had before met her jesting on such subjects—appropriate or inappropriate, as one received it. Most of us talk of our weeds and try them on with faces in accord with their coloring. Mrs. Duain did neither. As her eyes now met Annita's, the girl's lips parted in a distinct smile, sweet and natural and shyly affectionate. Her brown eyes (so pretty in color, but monotonous somehow to Mrs. Duain, used to her daughter's vivid face, and indeed to her own changing features as shown in her mirror) were shining a little. The light hair, too, seemed to lie more loosely, and therefore more acceptably to the older woman, who in her rich ripeness hated sleekness of any kind. They had passed a long evening alone to-gether family - wise, and after it as Annita stood there on the stair she seemed more one of them. There was a subtle loosening, not of the hair only, but of her whole being. Mrs. Duain decided quickly that the hour for action had at last come.

"We don't want to go to bed yet, do we, Helen?" she said. "Come in here with us, my dear; let's have a real hair-brushing talk. I never feel that I know a woman until I once brush my hair with her."

"But ought I to keep you, Mrs. Duain? Look at the clock."

The old hall timepiece was pointing to a late hour, yet Annita's hesitation was plainly more wistful than real.

"Oh, I did look at that old thing, and I looked right away again," said Mrs. Duain, waving both time and the reverend clock aside. "I don't want to remember how late it is. Go get your brushes and combs and wrapper and slippers, and we will have a real old-fashioned hair-brushing."

But with all her perfectly spontaneous and almost girlish charm of manner, Mrs. Duain was a determined woman of the world, with an object in view to attain and a resolute will to attain it within the hour. She was not thinking seriously of clocks, nor of dressing-gowns and slippers, and she showed that she was not when Annita returned burdened with toilet articles.

"Come here, my dear," she said. "Throw those things down on the bed and come here. Do you mind trying this on for me? I don't seem to be able to fit it on my own head"— which was not unnatural, as it was not for her head that Mrs. Duain had ordered the veiled bonnet. It fitted Annita admirably, as if it had been made for her — indeed it had been, with her own stolen bonnet as model.

21

"And now," went on Mrs. Duain, as one absorbed in her subject, "will you mind slipping this on?"

This was one of Helen's gowns, for which Annita had once stood as block, the girls' figures being sufficiently alike to allow this saving of Helen's overtaxed strength. A few moments later the cheval-glass reflected Annita's figure dressed in a full costume of perfectly fitting mourning, at which Mrs. Duain gazed with affectionate approval, half sad, half satisfied. Helen stood by, looking on with eyes wherein some mischief lurked. Her mother's careful schemes always amused the daughter. The two faces were reflected in the glass, one over each of Annita's shoulders, and as she chanced to glance from one to the other she stared for a moment, started, and then wheeled around with a little cry, half dismay, half question.

"My dear," said Mrs. Duain, soothingly— "my dear, why shouldn't you? Did you suppose I was ordering all these gowns and all these bonnets just for Helen and me? Aren't you my daughter, too? Won't you be one of us, dear? We were a little family of three. Let us keep that number."

But Annita had sunk down on the side of

the bed, leaning against the foot-board for support, her eyes dilating and fixed on Mrs. Duain, who went on with an unwonted nervousness under that insistent questioning look. She had not believed those light brown eyes capable of expressing such demand.

"I think it really best, really wisest, Annita, as—as you have already stayed with us this week. Of course it is for you to decide, but I think it far wiser." Annita looked down at the black gown, and her face seemed to close with a seal. Whether she wished to throw the gown off or not, Mrs. Duain could not at the moment tell, and for the thousandth time she wished the girl's face were more flexible. If it had been Jack or Helen, she could have unerringly read their inmost feelings in a moment. "Of course it is for you to decide," she repeated.

"Is it left for me to decide?" The question, the glance that went with it, were quick, almost stern, and Mrs. Duain, unaccustomed to sternness from any one, was too surprised to reply. Annita went on in set tones : "I heard you tell the doctor everything. I supposed you had to tell him, but have you told any one else ?"

Mrs. Duain actually stammered a little as

23

she tried to reply. She was thinking that this was not in the least what she had expected of the passive girl she had been watching through the week. Whatever else she lacked, there was plainly no shortage of courage. When cornered she would fight. But Mrs. Duain herself was a brave woman, and when she finally rose to the occasion it was to face fully the consequences of her acts.

"I am afraid I have made a dreadful mistake," she said, gravely. "My dear Annita, I am not, and I never have been, a very trustworthy woman in keeping a secret. I don't mean to break confidence, but I know I do. Now I shall have to ask a great faith of you when I say that until this moment I honestly did not know I was telling your secret. I meant to gain your permission first, but as I sit here and see you look at me in this way, I know that I have done and said things that were just the same as speaking outright. I am so distressed! I ask your forgiveness most humbly. I am ashamed to the quick ; but that doesn't undo anything."

Helen's daughterly impulse was to run to her mother and forcibly stop her humiliating herself before Annita Andrews. And yet, except for that intense gaze, Annita was not ac-

cepting the confession offensively. She seemed, in fact, to be scarcely hearing it. She was
now looking down and stroking the folds of
crape on the wrist of the unfortunate gown.

"Mrs. Duain," she said, more gently, "did the
woman who made this dress know?"

Mrs. Duain flushed. "I—I am afraid so. I
should have said 'No, of course not,' an hour
ago, but now—yes, my dear, I do remember in-
timating that you might be the one to wear it."

"Then that was why she told me her lover
was killed in the war?"

"I suppose so," said Mrs. Duain, miserably.
"I suppose she thought you could understand
better than any one else. She didn't mean to
be impertinent, I am sure."

"Oh no, I didn't think so. But she must
have thought me very cold. I never dreamed
she knew, and people haven't told me such
things as a rule." She paused again in the
same absent way, stroking the crape. "And
my aunt?" she asked, finally, with another
searching glance.

Mrs. Duain flushed at the question. Her lip
quivered. She was not used to being cate-
chised, but she still answered with a meekness
that flushed her daughter's face: "Yes, my
dear, there I did speak almost openly. You

must have known I would have to give her some explanation of your staying here."

"Then, I suppose, that was why she told me all about losing her first lover. I knew my grandfather sent some one away before my uncle came. And when my uncle came to see me he told me all about his first wife's death. I wondered why at the time. I never was told these things before. Do you suppose it's because I"—she looked up questioningly—"because they think I'll understand now?"

"Oh yes, dear," cried Mrs. Duain, eagerly— "yes; that's one of the compensations for letting others know of our sufferings. Nobody wants to tell anything to happy young things who can't really understand. You'll find all the suffering world open to you if you will only let it know that you have suffered."

Annita sat gazing into space. Her eyes had lost the stern look that questioned Mrs. Duain, and seemed to be ardently questioning all life.

"As I think of it, it seems to me everybody I have seen this week has told me something. Is that a sign they all knew?" She turned her eyes full on Mrs. Duain again. "Even your friends, people I never knew before, have talked with me. They wouldn't if they hadn't known all. I feel they wouldn't. Has every one who came near me been told—every one in the house, even the servants? Susan told me yesterday she was soon to marry the coachman."

"Oh, Annita," cried Helen, with deep offence, "how can you berate mamma so? I won't allow it. If she has done wrong, she's told you she's sorry."

"Being sorry doesn't put the wine back in the bottle, Helen," said Mrs. Duain, her voice quivering. "I have spilled Annita's secret, and she has the right to be angry."

Annita started as if waking from a dream.

"Angry! But I'm not angry." Her eyes filled with quick tears; her face flushed distressfully; she spoke hurriedly, with the pain of one utterly misunderstood. "Sometimes I think I must have frozen water in my veins instead of blood. I can't thaw quickly. I don't know how. I don't know what to say now—only—I do know I want to wear this—this dress, if you'll both let me."

The last words came suddenly and she rose, trembling with excitement, both hands appealingly out-stretched. Her changed attitude, the influence of the accepted mourning garb that draped her standing figure, the timid entreaty of her hands and voice, all drew Mrs.

Duain and Helen fluttering to her with an entirely new sense of womanly relation. The breath of a strengthening sentiment blew them together as the little whirlwinds draw up feathers ; and like soft feathered things, and with the prettiest nestlings, the two women, to whom caresses were the natural expression of feeling, drew near the one they were teaching to be like themselves. It seemed to Mrs. Duain that she could actually feel the girl changing and softening in her hands. She had a theory of her own that all womankind properly belonged to the dove-cote, and should wear their softness outside ; and though some, by a mischance, might come to wear their feathers inside, as a heavy casing confines a soft pillow, a little slit in the cover or a hard thrust would invariably discover that there were normal contents enclosed. Annita had received both slits and thrusts in this week, and the last experience of the hour had been a hard one. While she clung to them ·with a shy happiness and timidly gave loving touch for touch, she showed the strain she had suffered in the pallor that followed her excitement ; and Mrs. Duain, with tenderest motherly solicitude, carried her off to her room at last, not leaving her until she had seen her laid in her bed with her weary head on the pillow. As she bent over the girl for a last kiss, Annita flung her arm suddenly around her neck, drawing the kind face down to hers.

"Oh," she whispered, softly, "you don't know what you have done for me. I only began to live one week ago to-day, when you first took me in your arms."

It was more than a year and a half after Gettysburg, and therefore after peace was declared, when a warm summer morning found Jack Duain, as one risen from the dead, entering his native town. He walked slowly and nervously down the well-known platform, waving aside the whips of the same old drivers he had left there when he went away with his regiment. He knew every one of them, but not one recognized him, and, a little dazed at their blindness, he walked, still as if disguised, into the streets, with feet familiar to every stone that had stubbed his bare toes when, as an obstinate and hardy boy, he would distress his mother by running barefooted through the town. There was something uncanny to him in the way those he knew as he knew himself looked him over carelessly as a passing stranger; but after the first shock of surprise what he began to dread was that he should at last meet some one

who would know him and tell him news that
he longed for yet feared to learn. When at
last he reached his own house his courage
failed utterly on the door-step, and he turned
off without ringing the bell, but only to make
his way to the wicket-gate that closed in the
garden at the side of the house. Once in the
garden, he slipped from bush to bush as cautiously as when he and Helen had played hide-
and-seek there together as children, stealing
from behind the tulip-tree to the snowball-bush,
from the sweet-smelling shrub-bush to the
sweeter magnolia-tree. These old familiar
odors spoke to him of the past, and the old
childish haunts pulled at his heartstrings.
Even the air, kind and sunny, seemed the
weather he best remembered, and all combined
to quicken his imagination and make his heart
beat with foreboding. Human changes might
be waiting for him beyond this unaltered nature and within the unchanged stone and mor-
tar of the old house that rose before him. Were
strangers in the home? At last he paused
under the jutting bay-window of the low room
where in the old days he knew his mother and
Helen would have been sitting at this hour.
Here, crouched down like a thief, he listened,
holding his breath.

THE SIXTH SENSE

"My dear," came a clear rich voice floating out from the open window above him into the warm air, "I beg of you, don't open that umbrella in the house. I'm not exactly superstitious, but then—"

"Everybody knows it's too unlucky to open umbrellas in the house," said a lighter, because younger, laughing voice, like an echo of the old one.

"Open the umbrella out of the window, Annita, and mend it that way."

There was girlish laughter within, and then out came the closed umbrella from the smilax-covered window-frame. A woman's white hand followed, pressing the catch open and shaking and unfurling the silk. It was all so foolish, so simple and homelike and sweet, to the hungry ears outside. A great thanksgiving swelled in Jack Duain's heart. They were not gone, not dead, nor even changed. How often had he been warned by that same loved voice as to the unnecessary recklessness of opening an umbrella in the house! It was the old house, the old habits, the dear old superstitions. He had come back from the dead to find them all unchanged—all just as he left them, those he loved and those who loved him. They were not too broken either

31

by his supposed loss, for they could still laugh and jest as of old. For this last he had no resentment. He was in a moment like a boy again, and moved to surprise them as a thoughtless boy might. He rose softly to his feet, shielded by the wide-open umbrella. The waving ferrule seemed to him to be poking at him jocosely as the mender jerked it awkwardly back and forth. He caught it, and thrusting his shield above his head, was face to face with Annita Andrews.

There was an instant outcry in the room, a rushing to and fro, a tumultuous excitement, but the mother's voice was piercing to his ears through and above all. The appealing cry of a child on the mother's ear is most insisted upon, but there is a mother's cry as well, and whether he was dragged into the room or somehow scrambled in to where he might fall at his mother's feet and reach the mother's arms, the son could not have told. He only knew that he was there, and the long days and suffering nights were now as far in the past as all troubles had seemed when as a child he had cried out in the dark and waked to feel those same warm arms about him. He opened his eyes after a little and looked up to laugh at himself and at her, but tenderly.

"Don't look down on me like that, mammy dear; I'm all right now, and I was all right weeks ago, only I was afraid to come home. I didn't know what I might find, here. When I stood outside there and heard your voices— well, I always thought they were sweet voices, but I didn't know how sweet. Don't you want to know where I've been and what I've been doing ? I've died twice since I saw you, mammy dear."

He showed it all, Mrs. Duain thought, touching his face with gentle finger-tips, as if she scarcely believed it real. It was Helen who listened to the quick, dramatic account of the awakening from that first death on the battle-field, the chance succor by the enemy, the unconscious days, the months in a prison-hospital, the half-recovery, and then the long, hopeless days of prison life that followed. On these last he would not dwell. Through all ran the strain of a desperate, unremitting effort to get news of home, to send home news of himself—efforts which they knew too well had all miscarried. Last of all, half due to the prison life, half to his own beating at the bars, came a fever that seemed to kill again. Waking to life for the second time, it was to ask his own name, and as memory came slowly

back he learned that the war was over, peace
declared, and he himself, though free to go
where he would, had been only a troublesome
prisoner and a hospital number for so long a
space of time that after these troubled days a
return to life and home and family needed
first the question asked and answered, Is there
home and family left to receive the lost one?
This question he had come himself to ask, waiting beyond the time when his bodily strength
was sufficient, because he dreaded the possible
test on sick brain and weakened nerve if the
answers were fatally wrong.   All this Helen
learned, partly with tender questioning, partly
by listening with loving interruptions and exclamations of sympathy; but Mrs. Duain could
only listen vaguely, having actual brain-room
for no more than this joy of restitution.   Yet,
being above all a practical woman, if a mother,
she began gradually to grasp the wonderful
fact that her son had come back to her, even
more, not less, than when he left.   By the
time her knees had ceased to tremble under
the sweet pressure of his head, her keen eyes
had noted the stronger and nobler lines of the
irregular features, the firmer fold of the lips,
and the quiet strength of the steady hands
that had been so restless with life.   He was

34

thin, he was worn and weak, but the vigorous life was all there yet—there was nothing lost of the Jack Duain that had been, and much gained. He had left her a jocund boyish man, and he had come back jocund still, she hoped, but with a developed manhood. Her motherly pride swelled her heart. She had mourned him bravely as a hero dying for his country; there was a stifling joy in having him a hero still, yet alive, growing into this ripe manhood, and more than ever all her own. Then she was suddenly and for a moment sickeningly reminded that there were more ways of losing a son than those supplied by battle and sudden death.

"Didn't I see some one else here when I broke in?" asked Duain, and after a shock of quick recollection and a little struggle with herself, his mother stooped and kissed him, whispering :

"How selfish I have been! But I could only think of you at first. She must have run away. Helen—"

"Just one moment, mamma," begged the sister —"just one moment more all to ourselves. I want to tell Jack something, myself." She was standing before her brother with her hands clasped tightly, and with the prettiest air of embarrassment, both mother and brother thought.

"Don't you remember, when you thought you were dying on that dreadful field and you sent us that dear message by one of your comrades—Mr. Griffin?"

"Griffin, was it? I didn't remember which one I sent."

"Well—well—" Helen halted, plainly dashed by this extraordinary forgetfulness. Mrs. Duain assisted her, smiling:

"The message was four words in all, wasn't it, and one to Helen? It's taken Mr. Griffin a great many hours to deliver Helen's part of it to her, Jack. Yes, he's taking her away from us."

"He's doing no such thing, mamma. He will settle here; near you; he said so. And, besides—

"'A son's a son till he gets him a wife;
But a daughter's a daughter all the days of her
    life.'"

She smiled significantly at her brother, whose surprised and sincere pleasure in her news flushed her face happily. She listened greedily to all he could say in praise of the lover, whom he now vowed he had sent to her for no other purpose than the one he had accomplished.

"You didn't!" asserted Helen. "You said just now you'd forgotten whom you sent"; and they wrangled over the matter as they had always laughingly wrangled together. It was all so natural, all music to Mrs. Duain. She could have listened for hours, but her conscience was now awake, and her duty to another pressed upon her.

"Helen, you are not being kind, dear," she said. "You, of all people, ought to remember that some one wants Jack now, and Jack must be craving the sight of some one more than he wants us."

Jack Duain wheeled round from his sister's side, facing his mother.

"What!" he exclaimed.

Helen shook her finger at him with a little *moue*. "Oh, you needn't pretend any longer; and as I told you my secret, I do think it's mean of you—"

"Helen," broke in Mrs. Duain, "go and order some luncheon for your brother. He must need it."

"I don't," said the son, laughing. "But, if you want, Helen will go and look for that white horse you used to send us to look for when you wanted to talk with father. Won't you, Helen? That's what mother means. How good it is to be home and hear all the old songs!"

He was laughing, and so was Helen, but Mrs. Duain could only force a smile. She might have agreed with Helen in thinking Jack only desirous of concealing his love-affair from them, but that her quick ear had caught a sincerity of surprise in his hasty exclamation. She gave an earnest signal to Helen, who left them, at once sobered by the gravity of her mother's face. Mrs. Duain joined her son at the window towards which he had moved. He was looking down the street in a direction which a little relieved her anxious forebodings. It seemed to her as if one finger loosened of a hand that was clutching her heart.

"Yes," she said, softly, almost pleadingly, "that is where you used to find her. But now, dear, she is here more than there. Don't try to keep anything back from me. I know it all —and from herself."

She looked into her son's face as he turned it to her, and the finger that had loosened closed down again and tightened on her heart. They stood gazing at each other until the mounting terror in her mind spoke in Mrs.

38

Duain's eyes so plainly that her son answered it.

"Now look here, mother; I'm not crazy. I
didn't come home, and I wouldn't, until I was
sure I was all right, after the fever. But there's
something all wrong here somewhere. I pledge
you my honor I haven't the least idea of what
you are talking about ; but I don't think you
are crazy for that reason, and you mustn't
think I am."

He looked at her with a frank eye as sane as
her own. Though he spoke humorously, the new
and more serious strength of manhood which
she had recognized in his face was in his manner,
and so convincingly that Mrs. Duain put her
hands to her head, distrusting her own senses.

"Then who is crazy?" she said, despairingly
—"you, or I, or Annita Andrews?"

"Annita Andrews!" repeated Duain. "Annita Andrews!" There was now not so much
bewilderment in his tone as indignation at the
name suggested. "Why, I never so much as
looked at her seriously. She never interested
me in the slightest degree."

Mrs. Duain deliberately turned and sat down
again in her chair before she could reply. There
was something here for discussion that could
not be entered into in any casual way. Her

son drew nearer to her and laid his hand on her shoulder.

"What is it, mother?" he said, kindly. "Why are you so troubled?" In his voice and touch Mrs. Duain felt instantly that there was something stronger than either death or marriage which might again take her son from her—his individuality. Before he left her he had been charmingly independent of all but herself, manly and original to a fault, but the last word of influence had always lain with her. That, she now knew, was over forever. He had never been kind to her before. It had been his to be devoted, hers to be kind. As her quick brain leaped to these conclusions, she knew at the same time that, whatever fatal mistake lay behind this complication, it was too late for her to give up the girl who seemed to be its victim.

"What is it, mother?" said Duain, again.

And then, in a kind of despair, she opened her lips and told him everything, from the day of Annita's entrance into the house to the moment when he saw her under the umbrella at the window. As the threads of the story reeled off, Duain listened at first with evident astonishment, then more and more blankly. At last he rose, brushing his hands across his face as if wiping away cobwebs of belief that clung despite him.

"Wearing mourning for me! Living as my widow! Upon my word, I never heard of such a thing in my life! Don't tell me any more, mother. I shall begin to believe in it all myself. It's the most curious sensation! My widow! Can she be deranged?"

"No, she is not. None of us is deranged," said Mrs. Duain. A theory was forming in her own mind, which she was not yet prepared to advance, but every moment she believed in it the more. "There is a horrible mistake somewhere. What can you do?"

"Do! There is nothing for me to do that I can see. It's a most terrible complication, and the publicity makes it doubly hard to deal with. Of course I'll do all I can to make it easy for her; but, after all, the mistake—if we choose to call it so—has been entirely hers. I think the undoing ought to be hers also, don't you? What could have been her motive?"

Mrs. Duain's reply was indirect: "Then you wouldn't consider letting things stand as they are?" Her tone was wistful.

"Marry her! Why, my dear mother—" Duain checked his amazement at the suggestion, evidently preposterous to him, and went on more quietly, half smiling : "I confess that solution had not for an instant occurred to me. The affair is befuddling enough for a man of any imagination, but I never cared anything for the girl. Until now I never had any reason whatever to think she cared for me." He blushed as he spoke, then laughed at himself. "I'm sure I don't see why I should blush over it. Annita Andrews was not the kind of girl to stir my blood, as I remember her; but, as I say, it's a befuddling affair."

"She has changed very much," said Mrs. Duain, quickly. "And you didn't dislike her before. You visited there constantly."

"As every one visits everywhere constantly in a little place like this. But none of us were ever in love with Annita Andrews. You know that."

"I don't know why you shouldn't have been," Mrs. Duain replied, warmly.

"Neither do I. But none of us ever were. I don't believe she ever had a lover. For myself, I never cared to be with any girl in my salad days (they seem years back), unless I was sure several other men wanted to get her away from me. I don't think I was a very nice boy. And there was nothing of the siren about Annita Andrews. That at once prevented her being my type of woman. Why, mother, you know the girl was dry and silent as—not a mouse: mousy women have their attraction—she was more like an oyster. She was monotonous in her very good looks."

"She's more than good-looking. She has a lovely face."

"Oh no, she hasn't, mother dear; you are looking at her now with your own reflection thrown on her. She never had a lovely face at all. It was a handsome and totally blank countenance, and that's all. I've stood on her door-step time and again bored to death at the thought that I knew just how pretty she was going to be when I got in. There's no variety about her. I don't mind a woman being down-right ugly, if only she'll look handsome at times. There's some excitement about her then. You can stand on the door-step and wonder whether she's to look a fright or a brilliant beauty. There are girls like that."

"I shouldn't say your salad days were entirely over," said Mrs. Duain, dryly. "You've been dropping very naturally into the present tense."

Duain laughed.

"Well, all the old blood didn't run out on the field, I suppose. I thought it had. But,

43

you know yourself, if a girl has the looks and the position in life that Annita Andrews had, and still never a lover, there must be something extremely wrong with her."

"No, there is nothing wrong with her," said Mrs. Duain, rising to the challenge. "She was wrong without something, I'll admit. But, Jack, though you may not believe me until you see her again, she's gained that — that something—whatever it was that you missed. How do you remember her?"

"Oh, very well indeed—as a girl who ought to have been extremely beautiful and charming, and who wasn't either in the slightest degree. She missed both by an inch, for some queer reason. She reminded me of an Indian baby, somehow. I always believed she could swim if anybody would throw her into the water; but nobody wanted to take that trouble."

Mrs. Duain's eyes shone; she leaned forward in her chair.

"That's just what has happened. She has been thrown into the water, and she can swim now. You call it swimming; I call it gaining the *sixth sense*. Annita has been here constantly with us, and I have introduced her into the heart of our own little circle of friends. You know what they are—very different from

44

anything she was accustomed to, and calculated to develop any girl. She has been a great favorite with them, very much admired, and brought out of herself. I can see all the time that she grows more and more attractive; and not to men only."

"Men!" repeated Duain, with a laugh. "Then my widow is not inconsolable."

"She has been carefulness itself," corrected Mrs. Duain, instantly. "I never saw any young woman in her position more delicate or showing more feeling."

Duain looked at his mother, half laughing, half horrified.

"Mother! You are speaking exactly as if she had a real position to maintain and be careful of. Has the girl bewitched you? What do you expect me to do? How can I possibly think anything of the delicacy of a woman who comes to my mother and pretends I am engaged to her after I am supposed to be incapable of contradicting the story? I let you run on because I could hardly collect my own senses before this and think it all over. But I must tell you now, nothing would induce me to marry any woman, no matter what endearing qualities she has since shown, who could have once had the amazing effrontery to claim

45

me as her promised husband, when I never promised her anything of the kind. I can solemnly swear to you that there was never any engagement whatever between Annita Andrews and me, and I think I can safely add that there never will be."

But Mrs. Duain shook her head slightly, as one not utterly convinced.

"I have seen the girl day in and day out for more than a year now," she said, slowly, "and I have never discovered this indelicacy and effrontery you talk about. She has matured and ripened into lovely womanhood, and she has endeared herself to me—endeared herself very tenderly, Jack—and I tell you plainly it hurts me and makes me indignant to hear you speak of her in this way, exactly as it would to hear one of my own children falsely accused. As you say yourself, you were not a very nice boy. I never thought you were, in those matters, and if you remember, I often told you so. And it's all very easy for you now to speak of yourself as a boy when you went away ; but you weren't a boy. You were, or ought to have been, as much a man in a responsible sense as you are to-day, though you were not the fine, developed, self-contained man I see in you now."

The mother's pride rose above all other and newer ties, and perhaps her courage failed a little. "Oh, my dear, I am so proud of you; so proud of your courage, your sufferings, and the way you have risen upon them to be what you are!"

"I am a very unhappy man at the present mo-ment, mother," said Duain, gravely. "Won't you go on and tell me what you mean when you say I was not a nice boy?"

"Those were your own words," said Mrs. Duain, evasively.

"They sounded stronger in my mother's mouth. I know you can't think me capable of having been engaged to Annita Andrews and now denying it to you, but you must be think-ing something not very different, unless I en-tirely misunderstand you."

"I never said she spoke to me of a formal engagement," replied Mrs. Duain, half reluc-tantly. "I said she confessed to me that you had told her you loved her, and that she loved you."

She bent her eyes on her son's face; but it was not her questioning gaze alone that sent the blood flying up over his forehead. After that first flush and the start that accompanied it, Duain sat quiet, with knitted brows, think-

47

ing deeply, and evidently self - questioning. He turned a grave face to Mrs. Duain at last, and met her still questioning gaze with a shake of his head and a worried shrug of the shoulders.

"You are entirely right, mother. If I were on the witness-stand to-morrow I could not possibly swear that I never told Annita Andrews I loved her ; and the fact that I couldn't swear I hadn't said it as amorously to every other woman with whom I spent a considerable time wouldn't help me, I suppose. When a man's saying good - bye and thinking he may never come back, he says a great deal he would never say under any other less melting and irresponsible conditions. Not that I mean to excuse myself. Do you suppose she could have been so innocent as to take some such foolish trifling in earnest ?"

He was speaking whimsically, but there could be no doubt of his sincerity ; and when he added, "Of course if that has been the case, there is but one course open to me," Mrs. Duain's courage suddenly and wholly failed her.

Her son was her son, after all, and there is nothing the natural mother craves more for her children than that they shall have whatever they want.

"We know Annita never had any serious lovers to teach her what serious love-making was," she said, "and we know you generally do pretty thoroughly whatever you do at all. But I don't really see that we are called upon to totally sacrifice you to Annita Andrews's ignorance of the amenities that pass between young men and maidens."

Jack Duain sat looking at his mother with amused eyes. She reddened under his look.

"Amenities is a neat word," he said. "No, mother mine, it won't do. You know as well as I all that rings with hollow sophistries. You could hardly get through it. If I said enough to an innocent girl to let her think of herself as my widow all this time, she ought to have the fair chance of being my widow in earnest. If she's grown as attractive as you say, I suppose I can stand it ; and it isn't as if I cared for any one else—that I can have."

Mrs. Duain sank slowly back in her chair, her face growing white. Her eyes were full of a frightened consternation, and her lips set in a distressed curve. Her son looked at her and smiled.

"Did you think getting new wounds was a sure cure for old ones, mother ?"

"I thought," stammered the unhappy mother—"I thought— Oh, Jack! I don't know what I was about to say I thought. I only wanted to gain time. This is all growing too tragic. I had forgotten all about her. I ought to tell you she is free again. Her husband died not long after you left us."

Jack Duain's face had turned suddenly as white as his mother's. He rose quickly and walked away from her to the window, where he stood looking out. His mother watched him miserably. When he came back to her she tried to read his face, but his quieted expression and manner were impenetrable.

"You never liked her, mother," he said, calmly—"chiefly because she had the shocking taste to prefer a better man to me, I think. I fancy her choice justified itself. But all this is apart just now. We won't speak of it again. I must find out, if I can, how much I am responsible for Annita Andrews's position, and pay what I owe her. That's task enough for the time. I can't arouse her suspicions and—" He laughed as if he could not help himself, not because he was amused.

"How on earth am I to meet her? If I remembered how I parted with her it would be easier, wouldn't it? But there were so many partings, variously harrowing. I am afraid

50

you and I were right, mother: I was not a
nice boy. Isn't this a commentary on me as I
was, and a lesson for the bachelor future, if I
am to have one? Now, mammy, cheer up.
You can't look tragics into this, or dignify my
end of it. You have a sense of humor, even if
you are my mother. On my side it's only
utterly ridiculous. And I am certainly de-
serving any suffering or deprivations I may
get out of it. Any and all—I am not except-
ing *anything*."

He spoke the last word significantly, and
Mrs. Duain understood him.

"And then remember," he added, "I don't
intend to accept any consequences that I
didn't bring on myself. I shall test that fact
somehow, and very thoroughly. I don't know
how—but I shall do it. It seems to me now
that I am not playing the very ardent lover.
Didn't you say Miss Andrews was in the
house?"

Mrs. Duain rose with a sigh.

"I suppose I ought to go and prepare Annita
for something—I don't know what," she said,
with a tearful laugh. "Oh, Jack, isn't all this
dreadful? You've just come back to me, and
we've done nothing but talk of some one else."

Then they laid their necessarily imperfect

plans.   Mrs. Duain was to find Annita, and in half an hour send her to Jack, who would wait for her where he was, alone, and thinking out his best course of action.

"Go say your prayers for me, mammy," said Jack, opening the door for her.   "Gettysburg was play to this."

"I don't know what to pray for," returned Mrs. Duain from the doorway, with that touch of naïve humor which nothing could quite subdue.   "I don't know what I want for you or anybody else, now.   I am so confused."

And then she left him alone.

Confused !   If she was confused, it was nothing to his mental state, her son thought, as he tried to decide what line of action he should take.   Half an hour became as a thin thread of time between him and the necessity for a decision.   In a kind of nervous despair he resolved that he would best economize moments by considering one possibility at a time, and the first episode must be, of course, the meeting.   How was he to meet her ?

A door at the distant end of the room opened, the curtain before it lifted, and there under the lifted curtain stood Annita Andrews looking in at him.

Duain's first thoughts, passing like lightning

in his brain, were as purposeless and weak as our impulsive thoughts are humiliatingly prone to be. Yes, it was just as he had said. She stood there looking as handsome as he had known she must look, impassive as she always had looked, and the half-hour which he was to have had was unfairly denied to him.

Whether he or she moved first he did not know. He only knew that the curtain fell at last over the door, closing them in together ; that they met near the centre of the room, and he was holding her hand as an acquaintance might — as he then felt morally assured he must have held it in their parting — no more, no less. Something outside of himself checked him from going further, and as she spoke he knew it was she that held him back, not his own indecision.

"Then you don't know? They have not told you?"

Her eyes, with a quick glance, had questioned his face before she spoke, and she was already breathing deeply, as if with relief, before his slow reply came in words.

"Told me what?" asked Duain, with that curious reluctance of an honorable man to tell in exact words the lie which he is fully prepared to act to the limit. She seemed to ac-

53

cept this question as denial, as he meant she should.

"Then I have the chance to tell you myself first—and explain—no, I can't ever hope to explain it."

She was trembling so violently that common humanity alone might have moved him to support her with his arm, but he could only stand motionless and silent, waiting for her to speak further. Her hand still rested in his, but he knew that she left it there for needed support, and for no other reason. He felt himself brutally judicial, thus waiting for her defence. Yet there was nothing else for him to do. As her attitude seemed to ask physical support of him, that he gave her, strongly and kindly, as his nature would have prompted him to give it to any woman. He even shifted his arm a little, so that her weight hung upon his hand more heavily, and he saw that she felt the kindly motion, for her face flushed hotly.

"Don't be kind," she cried, sharply; "you don't know what I have done." Her voice broke off as if it were impossible to say more; but after an effort she went on, in low, rapid tones, which he had to bend his head to hear. "First—may I see you alone, quite alone, for a few moments? I have been hiding in there, in

54

the next room, like the thief I am. I hoped you would all forget me. I crept in here to see you as soon as I heard them both go. Can you spare me ten minutes now—and alone?" She glanced back again at the door of the room, as if dreading interruption.

"We are quite alone," said Duain, gravely. "No one will interrupt us. What have you to say to me?"

He saw her lips move, but not a word came. Her face flushed from brow to chin ; her eyelids lay heavily over her eyes. Duain had not seen her eyes fairly since she entered the room. He looked now at the curved lashes lying on her flushed cheeks, and wondered how it was possible that overwhelming shame could so find expression in two slender lines. Her eyelids fluttered painfully, as if trying vainly to rise. The words came at last with a quick rush ; but they came, and the courage of the effort, the set will behind it, appealed powerfully to the young soldier. He remembered Gettysburg again, and thought this girl's white face might have been that of some stripling near him in the last forlorn charge. That silent appeal to his own soldierly instincts was the plea best fitted to soften Duain as a judge.

"I—I am wearing this mourning I have on

55

for you—and—I have been letting every one think that you were my—my lover—you who never spoke a word of love to me in my life?"

As she ended she drew away from him, as if a spasm of self-scorn gave her strength; but still she could not face him; her face was buried in her shaking hands. Duain stood near her, as confused in mind as before her entrance. His position, though entirely different, was scarcely less intolerable. He felt, and gratefully, that a great weight was shifted from him. He had thought a delicate and difficult task, an almost impossible test of a woman and of himself, lay before him, and now he saw that none of all this was to be. He was fully exonerated. He had, after all, done nothing whatever to be ashamed of; but this shame under which another, and that a woman, cringed before him was almost as distressing to his generous nature. He was helpless to aid her. How could he, of all men, speak to her? What could he say? The burden he had lost was on the proper, if the weaker, shoulders, yet he somehow felt that he himself must have imposed it there. Now that he was in no way bound, he could afford to be generous, and surely there was nothing to hate or turn from in this stricken figure of humiliation hiding an

56

ashamed woman's face from him. After all, she was a woman, and had proved herself a brave woman ; both facts meant much to Jack Duain. He forgot his own wrongs in his pity. That they had played together as children added its argument of mercy, and moved outside of personal feeling he did what was probably the only possible thing to do under the circumstances. With one step he moved back from the awkward present to the past, to the simple manner, even the name, of their childish days of play together.

"Now don't be foolish, Annita," he said, practically; "you never used to be a crying girl. Come, dry your eyes, and let's talk it all over. Upon my honor, I can't see what it's all about, or how any of it happened ; but I know you can explain at least some of it. You must know I want to help you—for old sake's sake if nothing else." He drew nearer, and taking her hands as he might have taken Helen's, forced them gently from her face. "What have you been up to?" he asked, kindly and quizzically. "I never have thought of you before as a tricky girl." He looked down at her, smiling, and went yet a step further. "Not that you weren't perfectly welcome to use me as you pleased, alive or dead ; but why am I claimed when dead and so vigorously repudiated when alive? That's what rather offends me."

Then she looked up at him, but only as one too desperately degraded to hide longer. The acute suffering that pinched her features made Duain catch his breath and glance at her again, as the eye is sometimes caught by a look of suffering on a strange face held for a moment eye to eye in the accidental press of a crowded street. Annita had been, in spirit at least, little more than a stranger to him in the casual intimacy of their young past. She seemed to recognize his impulsive sympathy in his glance, and it braced her to self-control.

"I was not crying," she said, with a set quiet. "When a woman is ashamed as I am she doesn't cry. This is all very good of you, Jack, very kind and very like you, but—no, you can't help me. Nobody can. I have done a terrible thing, and I've got to suffer for it all the rest of my life. I don't want to shirk my punishment, but I do want you to know how strong the temptation was, and that I never, of course, never for a moment, dreamed my fraud could involve you. It never occurred to me that you could possibly be alive."

Duain broke in, half laughing, half expostulating : "Are you sorry I am, then? Was that what you were thinking of an old friend as you looked out at me under that umbrella? Why, Annita, this is little less than brutal."

Her eyes lifted reflectingly, and he saw them fully for the first time since their meeting, and saw, too, that he had made one mistake. Either she had never been so near to him in the past, or she had changed from what he remembered, in one respect at least. When she looked up, the whole face was lighted by her eyes. They were serious, thoughtful eyes, deeper and darker than he had recollected them, and extremely beautiful. They looked fully, yet as if unseeingly, into his as she replied, with that direct truth which comes sometimes with distress :

"I don't know. I think I hardly realize that you are really alive. I keep thinking of you as I have for the past year. You seem two people to me, one dead and one alive."

There was the possibility of a confession in her words, and Duain was but human. What lay at the bottom of this mystery he had not yet fathomed, and a not illegitimate curiosity awoke, urging him on.

"How have you been thinking of me for the past year, Annita?" he asked, and then something of softness in his own tone made him flush uncomfortably and filled him with dismay. As she saw his color rise, hers flooded her face in a blush of womanly resentment, so different from the flush of self-scorn he had seen there when they first met that Duain cried out, aloud, in self-abasement :

"No, no—don't think that. I'm not a conceited ass. I never thought you—that you cared for me at all." And yet he knew that he had been thinking something not very different.

"You mustn't apologize for anything," she said, with the dignity of real humility. "You have a right to think anything of me, but that one thing wouldn't be true. No, I never cared in the least for you in the way you mean. I hadn't even that excuse."

"I didn't consciously mean anything of that sort," corrected Duain, hotly.

He felt it a double grievance that he had let himself harbor such a self-conscious thought, and that it had been detected by Annita Andrews, who had not been too quick to read subtle shadings in the past. He began to feel of her as she had spoken of feeling towards him, as if she were two people—one, the shy, silent girl he had known ; and the other, this new and inexplicable woman, palpitating, flushing, and quivering before him, yet always self-controlled.

60

She went on, with the same quiet dignity, turning away from that side of the subject, and forcing herself to tell the whole of her story, though it could buy her nothing.

"And then, too, I knew that I was only wronging you — the dead, as I thought; by doing this, I knew that—" Her voice sank, she looked down at her hands, twisting her fingers together hesitatingly. "I knew that there was no other woman who might be wronged by it, because—"

Her soft voice broke off, she glanced up at him appealingly, and he finished the sentence for her with gravity and no disguise.

"Because you knew her well, and she told you that I had loved her?"

"Yes." She did not look at him, and spoke in hushed tones, as if intruding on some sanctuary. "You mustn't think she ever told me anything more; you mustn't think that. She only told of the bare fact and her distress that it was so. Did you know—" She looked up again, quickly, and he read plainly her first impulse to be a messenger, of new hopes to him, and then the more delicate impulse of present restraint.

"I knew that she was free again," he said, with equal gravity.

This seemed to him also no place or time for discussion of her. But was this the Annita Andrews he had known as utterly devoid of impulses of any kind? His mother had said she was changed, and she was right. Experience had greatly changed and softened her. He caught himself up with an effort, remembering that Annita Andrews had passed through no experience. The dead lover she had stolen, and mourned in pretence, now stood by her in the life, confessedly loving another woman, and to that woman's side she was almost sending him, apparently without a pang, indeed with ill-concealed eagerness. Duain would stand it no longer.

"I know you will think me unkind," he said, abruptly; "I don't mean to be, and I can't feel myself that I am; but we can't go on in this way, Annita. I feel like a man in a dream, and nothing is growing plain to me. I have been very ill, and perhaps that helps to confuse me, but I must ask of you some kind of explanation."

He stooped and took one of her hands between both of his, with kindly reverence, but no gallantry.

"I want to tell you first," he said, earnestly, "that I forgive you here and now everything, so far as I am concerned, sins confessed and unconfessed. But I do want to understand it all. Do you call that unnatural, Annita? It will be better for us both as things are, it seems to me. Come, sit here and try to remember how long we have known each other—forever. We went to school together, didn't we?" He drew her to a chair as he spoke, and stood by her with his hand on the back of another, as if waiting her permission to sit near her; but seeing that, despite his gentleness, she was again too agitated to take the initiative, he sat opposite to her, now plainly determined to probe the matter to the bottom, yet not unkind in his manner of insistence.

"You haven't left me a chance to flatter myself in any regard, you know," he said, encouragingly. "I begin to see that I was only a kind of peg for you to hang something on, and I want you to tell me what it was."

She looked up at him instantly, with a quick gleam of something like gratification in the dark eyes he found so wonderfully changed and softened.

"That was it," she cried, more naturally than she had spoken. "You have understood it yourself, as I didn't think I should ever be able to make you understand it; but you don't know, and I can't ever hope to make you know, how much hung on all this for me. You have always had affection, so you can't value it as I did. Every one cared for you. This whole town is mourning for you to-day as when you first—"

"First died," suggested Duain, with a laugh. But it was a laugh that only served to show he was strongly moved. "It's worth having died twice to know that," he added, with feeling.

"Would you be willing to live and suffer all the rest of your life as I must for having had one year of something like it?"

Duain turned sharply from his own emotion and faced the speaker, as if looking at some one never met before. Yet it was the same Annita Andrews. This woman too had monotonous fair hair, and features too regular for what he called beauty. She too was colorless, until she raised her eyes ; but those deepened, changing eyes altered and illumined the whole face, and the quivering mouth was as sensitive as a lovely flower. Her low voice, vibrating with passion and womanly longing, fell on Duain's amazed ears, stirring him profoundly. Bewildered, he looked once more for the brown eyes he remembered as shallow and

uninteresting, and again he met something so
different, so like a soul's revelation, that his
look fell before hers. He remembered suddenly, and with a strange vividness, how as a boy
he had once wandered alone into an unlit
church, and sat looking at the cold altar, at
the rigid chancel outlines, wondering with boyish intolerance at the rapt devotion of those
who knelt about him, straying in to drop a
prayer before this cold shrine. Then a little
door in the chancel had opened, and a white-
robed acolyte crept in with a lighted taper in
his hand. He touched the tiny flame here
and there about the altar, and instantly a soft
radiance sprang into life. The rigid outlines
grew into mystic holy places. The cold altar
had a being of its own, a strange sweet power
to call and claim, and, overtaken by the subtle
spell of the transformation, the boy's recep-
tive spirit had grown awe-struck and melted.
He remembered that he had involuntarily
bent his knees for the moment ; then, quickly
ashamed of this act of worship, so apart from
the faith of his own people, he had risen hurriedly and run from the church. This emotion of long ago was what he now recalled, as
he saw the soul of a woman rise and light Annita Andrews's eyes. In that moment he knew

E 65

what the girl he had known had lacked, and what had been gained by this woman who now was. That indefinable something, that flame of life which he could not name, but without which a woman was no woman to him, had, by some strange alchemy of life, been added to a seemingly sealed nature. The sixth sense of womanhood, his mother had called it, but the name mattered little to Duain. Whatever this gain was, with all its subtle charm and elusive beauty, he knew it was now Annita Andrews's possession, and he felt its power. As his quick imaginative brain worked to this end, Duain knew as instantly that a hitherto unsuspected danger lurked here for him. He was with a woman roused by himself, or at least through him, to a new and bewildering charm and claim of womanhood. In this bare fact lay enough to fire a colder nature, and he knew where his own weakness lay too well to trust himself. As in his boyish rush from the church, so now he felt—safety for him lay in immediate flight. He had stirred in his chair to rise and leave her, when Annita spoke again, and what she said made Duain sink back quickly, with the boyish flush of a self-detected coxcombry again coloring his cheek. Annita seemed either to have forgotten his existence as a part of the problem, or else she was speaking with deliberate intent to reassure him. Her excitement had gone, and she was again more like herself as he knew her first and best.

"I have never cared at all, not at all, for any man in the world. Perhaps it is because no man in the world ever cared for me. But how would you like to think, and have all your world know, that no one had ever felt it would be a happiness to spend the rest of life with you?"

She turned to him with the first smile of their interview, and for the first time her manner became that of the old childish familiarity, as his to her.

"You never suffered under anything like that. I always wondered why you weren't spoiled, Jack, but you never were conceited about women."

She spoke appreciatively and simply, and with a pretty grace of womanliness far removed from coquetry. Duain felt like hanging his head and confessing how nearly spoiled he had been about to prove himself regarding her. Plainly he need have no fear of capture here.

"Annita," he said, with a little laughing hesitation, "is it true that no man ever spoke a

67

word of love to you? Are you really so virgin a forest?"

She laughed also, with no offence or embarrassment, but with little mirth.

"If any one had told me a half-hour ago that I could be laughing here with you, I couldn't have believed it. You must have been very kind indeed, and good. I don't seem to be telling you all you wanted me to tell you, but all we are saying is bearing on it more than you know. And perhaps this is the easiest way, after all. No, I have never had a lover, nor a word of real love spoken to me, and I don't remember ever wanting either very much. You can't understand that, can you?"

She glanced at him with a little smile in her deep eyes, and, looking at her again, Duain repeated, with a wonder that was real :

"You never had a lover! But why not?"

Though the passing flame of passion that lit her face was gone, and with it the intensity which had startled him, he knew that he could never again look at her without a stir of memory, without seeing the possibility of that flame again lighting her features, just as the sight of a cold altar still invariably recalled to him the living vision of the one he had seen light to sudden radiance.

"Why not?" he repeated, as she did not reply.

She shook her head, with the same half-smile on her sensitive lips and in her eyes.

"You wouldn't have said 'why not?' a year ago. I have changed in this year. I know it. I see it in the mirror of every one's manner to me; even yours. I can't explain it, but it is so, and—oh, it has been such a happy year! I never wanted lovers, but I always wanted, passionately, to have what I have now. I mean I wanted to be able to attract and to hold people the way other girls did; not to hold men only, but women. You don't know what a shy, unattractive woman suffers, or how lonely it is, shut up in yourself. I was pitifully, desperately lonely. Not a soul ever cared to stay with me. I shall be more than lonely now. That·is the price I must pay for one year of this. The price I must pay!"

Her voice broke sharply in a sudden sobbing breath. Her face flushed and her eyes lifted exactly as Duain had seen a sudden physical pang flush the face and lift the bravest eye. She struggled for self-control, but the sob in her throat was followed by another and another. With a cry of helpless distress she broke down and covered her face with her hands. Duain bent forward and laid his hand on her shoulder.

"Don't cry so, Annita—don't," he said, helplessly. He had thought earlier it would have been easier for him if she had thus broken down. The courage and self-control he had admired had, he felt, hampered him, because it compelled his tolerance ; but this was tenfold harder. He had no stand-point left of the past or present from which to comfort her. With a confused impulse which he could not deny and did not stop to analyze, he bent nearer, and, with a quick motion, caught her and held her to him as if defending her.

"There is no price," he said, speaking rapidly. "Why should there be? No one need ever know anything. I don't know all that has happened myself, and you need never tell me. I trust you. I can't help trusting you. There has been some mistake somewhere, and I am willing to abide by it. Are you, Annita?"

She raised her head and stared at him, her tears driven away by her amazement. Though she did not move to withdraw from his arms, he knew it was only because speech and motion were alike paralyzed. He spoke again, with more feeling, as his eyes met hers. "The price is too heavy for you to bear, far too heavy. There will be none to pay if you marry me, Annita."

"I? Don't you understand anything I have said? There was no mistake. I can't pay too heavy a price for what I did. I went to your own mother and I *lied* to her." She put her hand to her throat as if the words actually choked her, but went on firmly, her face set. "She thought I said you were my lover, and I let her think I did say so, and I let every one think the same. I've stolen all the sweets of a loved woman, reaped all her privileges. You have no reason to pity me, Jack, no reason to sacrifice yourself to me."

Despite the sternness of her effort, she spoke with a simpleness, a sweetness and gratitude, that touched Duain deeply, and the soldier in him stirred again at her courage.

"There would be no sacrifice. I can see that now very plainly, and I could make you happy, I think. If you love me—"

She withdrew from him strongly, taking the leadership for the first time.

"I do not," she said, with spirit—"I do not love you. I thought I made that plain from the first. I tried to make it plain. I had no such excuse as loving you. And while I owe

71

you a great deal of reparation, you owe me
nothing—nothing at all—least of all yourself.
Now I beg of you—won't you listen to me a
moment? I will try to speak plainly and as
shortly as I can, and then go away forever.
This talk has been too long already. I came
in upon your mother just as she heard of your
supposed death, when she was suffering most.
I don't know what made me act as I did. I
was not apt to do impulsive things then. She
must have begun to influence me from that
moment. I have never been so influenced by
any one as by her. I never shall be again. I
cried there with her tears, and I trembled as
she trembled, until at last she turned on me
suddenly and asked me if—if I had better and
deeper reason for such grief than she. And
she said it so searchingly, with such clinging
caresses, such tenderness, that — I can never
explain it—but when I found my voice after
the first shock, that did stun me, I could no
more bring my tongue to say the word that
would separate us than I could have struck
her. Oh, you know how lovely she is !—what
it means to be loved by her ! While I waited—"
She paused, the great pain and difficulty of
speech returning. "It grew too late. Silence
was consent to her. Before I knew it I was in

her arms, on her heart. I have been there ever since. You are her son. You know all it means. At first I tried again and again to tell her, to confess to her, but that first day I was so frightened, so dismayed, at what I had done—I fainted ; and before I could undo anything, she had told, not only dear Helen, but the doctor. You know she is not very secret. And then others knew it—and then—I—I quite gave up trying to alter anything. Sometimes I suffered horribly. I was always afraid, but I was happier than ever in my life. I even let your mother think you had given me this ring — my grandmother's wedding - ring." She flushed deeply as she touched a ring on her hand, and went on less fixedly, more restlessly, flushing and paling by turns. " I don't know why these little lies humiliate me more than the great one, but they do, and that's why I want to tell you of them. I loathed myself each time, but not for long—I was so happy. I had never been with loving people, you know, and somehow every one was at once different to me. Helen told me first of her love-story. I was her lover's confidante all through. No one ever told me anything before. They all seemed to feel that I would understand them because I had loved. And I did understand,

73

but not for that reason. I could always have understood. It was what I was starving for, though I didn't know it. It was like a beautiful new birth. I never lived at all before this year. I was only a kind of sexless thing. You don't know what being a woman may mean to a woman. I never knew the privileges of real womanhood. I can't discuss or describe them, only they make a wonderful world to itself— and I'm glad—yes, I am glad I have lived in it. I know my way to it was a lie—and such a disgraceful lie!—and it only opened the door to me for one year, but—"

She paused, her tense voice quivering, and shivered slightly, as if in the chill of a reaction. Her words came slowly; her face was so white that Duain, watching her intently, stirred and quivering himself, was frightened at her pallor.

"I can never go back to just what I was. No one will confide in me—or ever respect me again—but I shall still be a woman—a woman, and always ashamed."

She rose and stood. Duain rose also, standing and looking at her as speechless as when they first met. He knew she was right. There was no deeper shame in the world than that of a woman shamed in her own sight and in the sight of other women. Men might forgive her this fatal mistake—he himself saw her temptation, her great and peculiar gain, ill-gotten though it was, and forgave her freely; but women, he knew, would never again receive her on equal terms. She seemed to have fully realized and faced this fact, and accepted it as her just punishment.

"I think I ought to give these to you," she said, quietly. "Your mother won't want to speak of them or to me when you tell her all I have told you. She has given me some things—treasures to her—that had belonged to you. Here they are. Will you take them to her?"

She drew out from her bosom a thin gold chain that held a miniature painted on ivory, a boyish likeness of Duain. Tied with it was a small gold pencil, which Duain also recognized as one he had always worn on his watch-chain. He still stood watching her, in a kind of horrified dismay, as she detached both tokens from the chain about her neck and laid them on the table near his hand. She seemed to attach no especial force to this part of her confession, though Duain did not move to take the tokens, but waited as before, his eyes intent upon her face. That a few moments back he should have gone so far as to be definitely de-

75

nied by her had filled him with amazement. He had been conscious of a sense of deep gratitude to her for the generosity of that denial. He had brushed near a danger, and escaped it by no good offices of his own, and yet recognition of the danger escaped could not restrain in him an unaccountable and overpowering desire to right her in his own mind at any risk. Something in the motion of her hand as she laid the tokens down forced a redeeming conviction upon him.

" You do care !" he cried, suddenly and warmly. " You couldn't have worn those on your heart for a year if you hadn't cared for them. It would have been horrible ! Don't you see, it would be horrible ; worse than all ! If you don't care for them, if you don't care for me, why is your hand still lying there by them ? Why don't you turn them aside as if they were common things."

If he could have recalled the hasty words he would have done so almost as they were spoken, for she lifted her hand with a start, as if the tokens scorched her, and laid it on her heart. It was no motion of melodrama. He could see her suffering, see her breast heaving under her palm as she pressed it down, as though trying to hold her body quiet by force while she thought. Her dark eyes began to stare at him pitifully, growing wider as with fright. At last, trembling and weak, she made one faltering step to fly, but her strength failed, and, with a little moaning cry of helplessness, she sank on her knees by the table, dragging the tokens desperately towards her, and hiding her face with them in her arms.

Duain stood looking down at what he had done, aghast and frightened. He dared not touch her or speak to her. He could interpret her emotion but one way, and he, and he alone, had done this much at least. But for him she would have gone out of his life quietly, and it might have been unconsciously as to her heart's secret. He had betrayed her to herself and before him.

How long he stood looking down at the motionless figure he never knew. If it were moments or if it were hours that framed his resolution he could not have told. He only knew at last that he blindly followed a struggling impulse, stronger than he dared resist, when he knelt down by her side and touched her hair softly, rousing her.

"Annita," he asked, gently, "was I right? You do care?"

She raised the whitest face, the most wretched eyes, he had ever seen. Emotion seemed exhausted in her, but his heart beat fast and thick as he again saw her face lit with the repressed passion of despair, but even so lit again to a beauty that caught his breath. It was more than the siren charm he had demanded of all women in his past. It was the charm of a delicate womanhood matured by living, suffering, sinning perhaps, but growing always into something finer, more uplifted, more forceful and possessive of life—like the wind - flower that in the spring sends up its pure frail blossoms to be swayed by every wind of the earth, while below are the vivid, time-colored leaves of last summer's growth. She had changed as he now knew he had changed, both watered by tears of blood, but she had put forth delicate blossoms under that wintry rain.

Had he?

Another face rose before him—the sweet siren face that had gayly ruled his youth and haunted his soldier days, and with the rising vision a great tumult began for him, a great inward dismay and distress. Strive as he might, the light of that sweet, long-loved face was only as the petty candles of a gay booth by the deeper lights, the altarlike radiance,

78

the white passion, of this despairing face, to which he had turned, he believed, only in pity and generous compassion. Was this new sense of reverence his blossom of new growth?

He stood speechless, and she pushed the tokens from her, not looking again at them or at him.

"Oh, why did you teach me this? Wasn't my punishment enough? I might never have known!"

"You must have known it sooner or later; and isn't it better to think that you were not playing a part all this year? Haven't you less shame, knowing that?"

"Yes," she answered. She rose, refusing his aid. "Yes, it is less ugly this way, and I don't suppose I shall suffer much more than I must have suffered."

Again she paused, and again the low voice, deep with the effort of speech, painfully sweet with feeling, stirred his heart bewilderingly.

"I would rather have you know that I never wore those on—on my heart until I felt a real tenderness for them. I thought I felt it because we talked of you so constantly, and I thought it was only a vague hero-worship. Oh, why should I try to make you understand, when I don't understand myself! I only

79

know that I never, never for one instant, wore them thinking of you as alive, or associated any such feeling with you as a living man, until— Oh, believe that much, won't you?"

She lifted her hand, which had fallen to the table, and without that support stood unsteadily.

"I don't think I can talk any more, just yet. If you could get me to my room without seeing any one, and then—home. I want a place to hide. When I am a little stronger I will write to Mrs. Duain. I can never see your mother again."

Her mouth quivered with the last words.

"You will see her often," said Duain, gravely. He went on slowly, as if feeling for words, or letting that same sure, slow-moving impulse prompt him :

"This can't end so, Annita. Don't you see it is impossible? Can I forget you after this? Can you forget me? When I spoke before it was under excitement. I know I only half meant it. But now—if you love me — *as* you love me—"

"Don't !" she cried, throwing out her hands and shrinking back. "I can't stand this. Not your pity—it stung before, and now—"

She stood trembling from head to foot before him, and with a quick motion he took her strongly, almost by force, into his arms. He drew her head upon his breast, holding it where he could look down on her face. In it, in the deep, startled eyes, in the quivering question of her sensitive mouth, in the exquisite flush of her unbelief, he seemed to be reading the key to his own conduct, his own assured impulse—explicable only in that moment to himself.

"But now—" he repeated slowly, almost as if thinking aloud. "No, no, this is not pity—not pity at all. It is reverence—love."

UNCLE ELIJAH'S CORNER CUPBOARD

"WELL, it can't be helped, girls, and there's no use crying over it."

"That's exactly why we are crying, Joseph. If it could be helped, there'd be nothing to cry about. Are you sure Uncle Elijah means Penniniah too?"

"I'll tell you just what he said. He fixed his face like this, and he crossed his hands on his stomach like this, and he said, way down in his throat: 'Joseph, there's no use arguing with me any more, and don't you dare to let Annie Tousey come here to try to talk me over. She fooled me once, and the same person don't fool me twice.. You tell her, from me, that the farm you are living on is mine—she never rested till she sold it to me—and now I'm going to rent it to another party. You tell her that I invite her and Penniniah and *their* husband to come and live with me, and that's a fair offer. Somebody's got to take care of the old man, and that's the only way this old man's going to be taken care of.' "

"Upon my word!" exclaimed Penniniah, scarlet with indignation. But Joseph's wife threw down her handkerchief from her face, and laughed through her tears.

"*Their husband!* Did he honestly say that, Joseph? Don't be so silly, Penniniah; it's only Uncle Elijah."

"I think it was the height of impertinence," answered Penniniah, loftily, and her sister laughed again.

"Well, Pen, we bring it on ourselves. Joseph calls you 'honey' and me 'dearie,' and you keep the linen-closet and I the pantry, and you make the cake and I make the butter, and I darn Joseph's stockings and you mend his linen, and I guess people do laugh at us; but I don't care if they do. You care so much about everything, Pen."

"He said something worse than that, Penny." Joseph loved to tease his sister-in-law in a good-natured way. "When he was talking, and talking to me about its being my duty to come and live with him, I said: 'See here, father, what about the girls? You don't want me to leave them, do you?' You know how he works his fingers over his face when he's going to say

83

something hateful? 'Well,' he began, brushing his nose down like this, Pen, 'when I invited the girls' husband to come and live with me, I meant the girls too, of course. Husbands embrace their wives, don't they?' "

Again Penniniah bridled in her anger, and again the wife laughed. " The horrid old thing! Pen thinks that's dreadfully indelicate, Joseph. She won't laugh. Never mind, Penny; we'll talk about something else. How are our chickens, Joseph?"

" Dead."

" Dead? Why, what do you mean? They weren't dead the last time I was over there."

" Wasn't our agreement that we should supply the eggs, and father set his hens on them and feed the chickens? We were to have a third of the results, weren't we? Well, it's been a poor chicken year, and all of ours are dead."

" But, Joseph—"

" Well, dearie?"

" Joseph, do be serious. How many of the chickens are alive?"

" Just father's proportion exactly. Ours are the dead ones."

Joseph threw back his head and burst into long and loud laughter, but this time his wife

did not follow his mirth. She put up her handkerchief to her eyes with a gasp of distress.

"Oh, Joseph, how can we ever live in his
house? He's dreadful! If he'd only come
here to live, it would be our house, and we'd
have some control."

"Don't you suppose father knows that as
well as you do?" answered Joseph. "That's
just why he won't come."

But Annie was now past laughter, and Joseph
rose and went towards his wife to comfort her.
"Now, Annie, don't you give up. It's not
like you. You never give up. He's my step-
father and he's your own uncle, and we've got
to take care of him somehow; but don't you
worry. You thought out a way to manage him
before, and perhaps you will again."

Mrs. Joseph, her face still hidden, shook her
head despondingly.

"That's the reason I can't do anything now.
He's as suspicious of me as he can be. He's so
stupid, he's on his guard if I only say 'Good-
morning, Uncle Elijah.'"

"That's not stupid; that's business, Annie.
You fooled him once, and you'd fool him now
if you got the chance—you know you would.
He has to be careful with you. Father's no
fool; I wish he were."

Mrs. Joseph lifted her face, shaking the tears from her eyes as she did so.

"Well, it's still summer, and we won't borrow trouble. If we can put off settling this until Christmas, we will. Didn't you say he was willing to wait until Christmas, Joseph?"

"Yes, indeed," said Joseph, indulgently. "We've a long, cold autumn to think it over in." His blue eyes twinkled as he looked up. "I don't mean to be parricidal, Annie, but if father was buying himself to keep till Christmas, he'd insist on a discount. What do you suppose he was doing when I saw him last night? Eating mushrooms for his supper."

Mrs. Joseph turned sharply. "Joseph, you didn't eat any?"

"No! He offered me some to bring home to you, but I told him I'd had too much trouble getting my family together, to run any such risks with it. Poor old man! He was eating away with the ends of his teeth, scared to death all the time for fear of a stray toadstool."

"They won't hurt him," said Mrs. Joseph, resignedly. "He's been eating them ever since he read in the almanac that 'many a nutritious mushroom meal goes to waste in the fence corners of improvident people.' There's another trouble if we go to live with Uncle Elijah. Jo-

86

seph, I cannot and I will not eat mushrooms, and Pen won't, and you sha'n't. How he manages to live on the things he does I don't see— mushrooms and pusley greens and stuff! He insisted on the fat and the cream of everything when he was a young man. Grandmother used to say she liked to cook for him, because he didn't eat just for hunger — he loved food. Dear me! what a table she did keep! I don't believe she spent much more for food than we do, Pen, but— Do you remember her gumbo soup? I put up a lot of gumbo this year, but our soups won't be anything like hers. It seems to me I can taste her gumbo soup now."

"Can't you follow her receipt?" asked Joseph.

"Receipt! She never had any that we ever saw. Grandmother just seemed to have cooking in her finger-ends. Poor Uncle Elijah! I remember, when he first went to house-keeping, he used to try so hard to have dishes like grandmother's. But grandmother always said she hadn't any rules in cooking, and your poor mother—"

"Lord! I can remember all that," interrupted Joseph. "Mother used to come over here and cry and beg grandmother for just one receipt. No use. She always said she hadn't any receipts, but mother never believed her. I guess father got his obstinacy from grandmother."

"I think that was awfully mean of grandmother," said Mrs. Joseph. "Uncle Elijah must have gotten his love of good eating from her too. And now he eats things I wouldn't set before the hired hands."

Joseph summed up the situation. "Oh, he hasn't always been as bad as he is now. He always loved his stomach and his pocket-book, and when he found mother and the cooks he hired after she died *couldn't* cook like grandmother, he just gave up his stomach to his pocket-book. That's about the sum of it."

"If I had some of grandmother's receipts, I'll wager I could cook almost as well as grandmother did," announced Mrs. Joseph. "It don't take much but a few good receipts, and common-sense, and liking good things to eat yourself, to make a good cook. I always did like good eating, Joseph. Indeed, I couldn't eat at Uncle Elijah's table. As I sit here it seems to me I can think of first one thing and then another that I couldn't stand, and Uncle Elijah wouldn't have anything changed to suit us. We are just beginning to get ahead with our farming and making it pay, and feeling so independent. Joseph, he must come here to us."

"He won't do that, Annie. There's no use worrying yourself trying to make him. Father never does what he doesn't want to."

Penniniah had not spoken for some moments. Now her voice rose, and in it was the ring of an inspiring faith.

"But, Joseph, Annie might make him want to, mightn't she?"

Mrs. Joseph turned her face quickly towards this faithful believer in her power. As she did so her eyes slowly grew reflective.

"Yes," she said ; "that's the way I managed him before. Uncle Elijah said he wouldn't buy this house at our price, you remember. I made him want to do it, and he did it, and perhaps we can make him *want* to come here to live."

Joseph looked up with a sidewise glance of humor. "Moving father is somewhat of a job to contemplate, Annie. If anybody can do it, you can, but I wouldn't set my heart on it. Do you remember that big old bowlder down at the end of father's farm, near the county road? Some people from the city came driving out one day to ask father to sell that bowlder to them. They wanted to dig it out and move it to their family burying-lot, as a tombstone for their father. They said he'd often seen the bowlder from the road, and always admired it. It's about as big as a house. Father told them they could have it—at a price, of course—and then he made one of the few jokes I ever heard him make. 'You can have it if you can move it,' he said (which he knew they couldn't), 'but, ladies, I should think you'd find it something easier to move your father.' Now, Annie, you can work that around to suit this situation. I should think you'd find it something easier to move this stone - house to your Uncle Elijah than to bring him to it. What do you say, Pen?"

But Pen was still gazing with the eye of faith at Mrs. Joseph.

"If anybody can move him, Annie can," repeated Penniniah.

"The question is, can anybody move him?" replied Mrs. Joseph. "Well, as Joseph says, we've a long, cold autumn to think it over in, and I promise you I shall think hard."

Despite the mushrooms so dutifully and economically eaten, if (according to his stepson's suggestion) old Mr. Elijah Tousey had bought himself at a discount on a question of longevity, he would have made a good bargain. Indeed, by the time the Christmas season came around, the old man seemed somehow to have obtained a renewal of his lease of life and vitality. He had been obliged to use a horse and buggy whenever he wished to go any distance from his farm—an extravagance that tried him sorely ; but now it was observed that he was returning to the habits of his youth, making his feet do a horse's duty for him. Joseph's home was some miles distant from Mr. Tousey's farm ; but on Christmas morning, to the amazement of his nieces and step-son, Mr. Tousey was discovered walking up the road that led to their house. The paths had not yet been cleared, and the old man, stick in hand, was sturdily breaking his way through the light snow that had fallen in the night. Mrs. Joseph, sitting at the head of the breakfast-table, saw him first.

"Goodness !" she cried, dropping her knife and fork on her plate, "here comes Uncle Elijah ! Penny, you go and open the door for him. If I meet him at the door, he always looks at me as if he'd caught a hypocrite, and if I don't meet him he isn't any better pleased. Of course we've a better breakfast and a later breakfast on the table than we ever have. He never keeps Christmas, and he don't see why any one else should. Joseph, can't you hide those chops ?"

"'Tain't worth while," said Joseph, easily. "Let him see something to find fault with right away. It'll save him the trouble of hunting. Sit down, dearie, and pass the coffee. Pen, bring your uncle Elijah right in here. Merry Christmas, father! Have some breakfast?"

Mr. Tousey stood in the doorway and looked over the table. He had once been a tall, eagle-faced man, with a hooked nose and erect bearing, and somewhere back in his youth had possibly been called handsome. Now, from his roughly shod feet to his thick gray hair, down the whole line of his bent figure, he had not one pleasing feature, with the exception of his eyes. These were dark and piercing whenever he opened the two gray-lidded boxes that closed them in, but, as a rule, the bushy gray eyebrows fully concealed this one remaining apology for personal appearance. He spoke as if he found his pleasure in a satiric mode of address.

"Breakfast! Humph! Mine was over at six o'clock. Bacon and cold bread. When Elijah works for Elijah, he rises early and he works hard. I came over to look through my farm accounts with you, Joseph, and talk over some other business. I won't interrupt your breakfast. When you get leisurely through—

leisurely through. No; I haven't eaten a bite away from my own table in these fifty years— not for fifty years. If everybody ate at home there'd be less trouble in the end. One meal taken out breeds three to be given in. No; I only eat at home. Annie, there's something in the old attic here I want to attend to. I'll wait for you there, Joseph. I don't need any showing about this house, Penniniah. I lived here before you were born."

"Hateful old thing!" Mrs. Joseph was saying, amiably, when Penniniah came back from the hallway, where she had gone in a futile attempt to politely point out the attic stairs. Penniniah was flushed, and complained, in an angry whisper :

"I declare, I don't know why it is. I know you have the farm rent all ready for Uncle Elijah, Joseph, and I know your accounts with him are ever so much straighter than his with you — all our chickens dead, indeed ! — but, I vow, when he looks out at us from under his eyebrows I feel exactly as if he knew we'd been tampering with the farm accounts, and as if we were behind with the rent."

Mrs. Joseph laughed comfortably, eating her muffins and chops as if Uncle Elijah were not.

"You always were too honest, anyhow, Pen,"

she said. " Joseph, do you know, she once bor-
rowed a dress of me to wear on a two days' visit
in town—we never had clothes enough for both
of us—and when she gave me the dress back, I
found she had added some new laces on the
bosom as a kind of dress rent. Did you ever
hear such nonsense? She said she 'felt more
comfortable.' I never was like that. I never
remember feeling so comfortable as I was the
day after I fooled Uncle Elijah. What worries
me is, I'm afraid Uncle Elijah came over here
to open that question of our living with him.
He's been so well this winter, I hoped he'd forgotten about it. Do you think he's come for
that, Joseph ?"

"I know it," replied Joseph, calmly ; "I saw
it in his eyes. Father never gives up anything,
Annie."

"Joseph ! Penniniah ! What was that ?"
Mrs. Joseph was not a nervous woman, and was
pre-eminently a woman of action ; but, with
the other and less active members of the household, she sat petrified at the breakfast-table,
stunned for the moment by what was first an
indistinct rumble, then a thunder-like noise,
from above.

"It's Uncle Elijah !" gasped Penniniah. At
the same moment her sister and Joseph roused

to action. They were both out of the door and
half-way up the stairs before Penniniah crossed
the threshold. It was Annie who reached the
foot of the attic stairs first, and when Joseph
joined her it was to find her standing checked
and bewildered, gazing up.

"Uncle Elijah!" she was calling, tremulously.
"Uncle Elijah! Oh, Joseph, you call him!"

"Father!" thundered Joseph's alarmed voice.
"Father!" There was a dead silence above
them. "What is that?" asked Joseph, pointing up the stair. But Annie could not tell
him.

Half-way down the narrow stairway—one
end edged upon a step, the other end complete-
ly blocking the trap-door that opened into the
attic—lay a curiously shaped wooden obstruction.

"Uncle Elijah," quavered Annie again, "do
tell us where you are! Joseph, I believe he's
under that thing!"

An angry, rasping voice made its way to
them past the obstruction.

"Don't be a fool, Annie. Don't you know
a corner cupboard when you see it? Of course
I'm not under it. It's my own, and I wanted
to get it out of the attic, and it's stuck somehow. You and Joseph pull when I push. My

95

soul! when I was young I knew how to work. Pull, can't you?"

But Joseph and Annie either could not or would not pull. They only stood looking at each other.

"See here, father," called Joseph. "I don't doubt the cupboard's yours, but why in the world didn't you tell us you wanted it, and ask us to have it taken out for you?"

There was an ominous silence from above, and then, as always when he wished to be most aggravating, Mr. Tousey ignored his step-son's existence, speaking over his head to his wife, as if she alone had any intelligence.

"Annie Tousey, are you there? Then will you kindly," asked Mr. Tousey, with icy civility —"will you kindly open the lower door of this cupboard? The one down there by you, if you please."

There was the sound of a key turning in a lock, then a smothered exclamation from Mrs. Joseph. As she unlocked the door of the cupboard, the door being on the lower side, the contents had poured out on her head, burying her in a kind of magpie collection of baby-clothes and short-clothes, small shoes and large shoes, boy's clothing and lad's garments, man's hats and coats and waistcoats. At least one speci-

men of everything that goes to clothe humanity up through the seven ages of man was there.
Joseph brushed the articles aside and pulled his
gasping wife out from the mass as Uncle Elijah's voice came down to them again.

"Perhaps you'll believe the cupboard's mine
now, Annie Tousey. This cupboard ought to
be full of my own clothing. My name's on every piece of them—or it was when I left them
here. I packed them away in here as I outgrew
them. Your grandmother gave me the cupboard before any of you were born or thought
of. I forgot to take it away when I married.
If Joseph has any more doubts—"

Joseph was turning over the clothing, whis-
tling softly and shaking his head.

"Annie," he whispered, "ain't this awful?
And his own baby-clothes, too, mark you! To
think he ever was a baby! Say, father, don't
you worry any more about proving possession.
Annie and I know these things are yours. We
don't want them. Lord! Annie, he might as
well have thrown us down his photograph.
These couldn't belong to anybody else."

Annie, with an awe-struck expression and gingerly fingers, was also turning over the articles.

"Indeed, Joseph, I never saw anything so
pitiful in all my life. And these innocent

little baby-clothes, they make me want to cry. Penniniah, do look at these things. It's been a long robbery of the poor. Poor Uncle Elijah!" Penniniah stood at a little distance, watching the inspection.

"It's so dreadful even Annie can't laugh at it," said she, in the same awed whisper her sister had used; and then Mrs. Joseph did laugh, but it was an hysterical sound, interrupted at once by Mr. Tousey's sarcastic voice from above them.

"Joseph, when you all are good and ready to help move this cupboard, I'd like to have it done, and get out of the attic and go home. I know it's only kind of wedged on the lower step down there. Lift it up and let it down easy. I'll hold back on it."

Mrs. Joseph hurried to one side of the cupboard as her husband moved to the other.

"Do be careful, Joseph. It's awful to have a heavy thing like this chase you down the steps. Uncle Elijah can't hold it back."

"Well, he seems to be doing it," said Joseph, rising to wipe his brow after a fruitless effort to lift the cupboard. "Father, can you hear me? Let her go up there."

"I'm not touching her," growled the cupboard's owner. "Why don't you pull?"

"Wait one moment," said Mrs. Joseph, who had been examining the stair. She had climbed up the narrow steps as far as the space allowed, and, clinging to the cupboard's edge, looked up at the low stair ceiling. "Why, Joseph, it isn't stuck at the bottom at all ; it's stuck up here ! Don't you remember grandmother had these attic stairs altered? It must have been done after the cupboard was taken up. It'll never on earth get down through the trap-door. We'll have to push it back and get it out of the windows. Uncle Elijah, we've got to get the cupboard back in the attic before we can get it out. You lift it up, and we'll push it. Now, all together when I count three."

Since the memorable day when she had out-witted him, Uncle Elijah had continued to pay certain tribute to his niece in the shape of a sarcastic but marked respect for the wisdom of her declared judgments. Now he did not for a moment question her decision. They could hear evidence of his obedience in his groans of effort. Those below were not idle. Penniniah lent her hand, and Joseph and Annie worked in concert, but the cupboard remained immovable.

"There's only one thing to do," panted Mrs. Joseph, drawing back at last. "Let go the cupboard, Joseph. We're wasting time and strength, and not moving it an inch. It's so jammed, Uncle Elijah can't lift it, and we can't possibly move it down past the top of the ceiling, because it physically won't go. The only thing to do is to saw the cupboard in two, and then we can pull the pieces down and let your father out. We can put the cupboard together again so you'll never know it's been taken apart, Uncle Elijah. Get the saw, Joseph."

"Joseph, don't you do anything of the kind," commanded Mr. Tousey. "Annie Tousey, anybody 'd think you were made of money, to hear you talk. You can't make kindling-wood out of my furniture. I guess I'll find a way to get this cupboard down, and without waste, either. If I don't, I'll stay here till I do. What's that, Annie? No, don't you go calling in any help from the neighbors. I ain't going to be taken out of an attic window as a free circus for all the boys in the country round. You can all go away from down there and leave me. I'll call you when I get ready to make a move. No, it isn't any worse to be shut up Christmas day than any other day. You'll see I'll think of a way to get me out that ain't window or door. Annie Tousey, you used to have a head on your shoulders. You can be thinking too, if you get time. Do you hear me?"

"Yes, Uncle Elijah," called back Mrs. Joseph, but it was in the voice of one roused from deep absorption. She had been again turning over the scattered clothing on the stairway, and now she rose and faced her husband and sister with a light of prophecy on her face. In her hand was a small fat volume of manuscript leaves. As she held it open, the leaves showed stained and old and thumb-marked.

"Children," whispered Mrs. Joseph, solemnly, "this is grandmother's receipt-book! She must have kept it hidden in that old corner cupboard in the attic. I know now exactly what I'm going to do. There isn't any way for Uncle Elijah to get out, and the Lord has delivered him into my hands."

The old attic in which Mr. Tousey suddenly found himself prisoner was one of those spider-haunted, quaint-raftered garrets that belong in old houses. At either end of the hipped-roof was a window, and in at the east window the sun shone with that dusty brilliancy that motes lend to sunshine. There was very little furniture of any kind in the attic, and no chairs, though the old gentleman sought for one diligently. Neither were there any objects of in-

terest stored here to divert the mind, except
the one corner cupboard, which Mr. Tousey had
already partially removed. It seemed, therefore, that a Christmas-tide of some dreariness
was ahead for the prisoner, unless he bent his
pride and called in the help of the neighbors, which, judging from the uncompromising
frown that had settled on his brow, Mr. Tousey
had no intention of doing. He spent the
greater part of the forenoon pacing the floor
back and forth, his brow bent, his hands behind
his back, now pausing at the shady west window
to look out on the fields of snow, now at the
sunny east window to look out on the trees
that the winter sun was rapidly divesting of
their snow robings. It was about twelve o'clock,
his dinner hour at home, before Mr. Tousey
condescended to improvise a chair for himself;
and when he did finally decide to make an old
pig-skin-covered trunk, that he pulled out from
under the eaves, do duty as a seat, he sat down
upon it very wearily. The garret was not cold,
for the weather was not piercing, but as soon
as Mr. Tousey ceased his walk he felt the chill,
and rose to find a remedy. As a son of the
house, he knew that a large register in the
attic floor led to a warm room below, and this
register he immediately sought and opened.

As he did so he glanced down casually into the room beneath, then stood motionless, peering through the open iron-work, his brow contracting, his neck lengthening as his interest grew. This room below was, as he knew, the guest-chamber, and though no one was then present, he could see that some one had lately been there, for all the guest-room furniture had been drawn back against the four walls, while in the cleared centre of the floor was set a large table, spread as for a Christmas banquet, with Christmas wreaths and holly on the board, and with four covers laid, one at each of the four sides. As he noted these details, the old man's astonished stare turned slowly to a more and more keen glance, and at last he began to nod suspiciously to himself. A grim smile spread over his features as he half shut his eyelids, standing there thinking. Finally he stooped, and, lifting the register bodily from its setting, disclosed the open hole, through which, kneeling with difficulty on his stiff knees, he thrust down his old white head for a closer inspection of the room below. He rose at last, flushed and trembling with his exertions, and set back the iron-work softly, carefully closing the register again.

"Annie's up to some of her tricks," he said,

as he returned to the pig-skin trunk. " I guess I'll wait a bit and see what happens."

Nothing happened for several hours, and as he sat there waiting Mr. Tousey began first to doze a little, with his head back on the bare rafters, and then to grow singularly restless, with a restlessness which was more than the ordinary impatience of waiting. Now and again he lifted his head and sniffed the air with the look of one trying to place something half forgotten, and once he brought his hand down on his knees with a slap of decision, as if he had identified what he had been seeking to place. As time went on the most untrained nostrils would have detected delectable suggestions in the unseen, impalpable, but none the less richly freighted smoke that came floating up into the attic. The merest novice could not have mistaken for anything but baking gingerbread the hot gingerbread waves of air, and roasting turkey and frying oysters and bacon were no less unmistakable in their aroma. But there was a something in this hearty atmosphere that seemed each moment to more and more bewilder Mr. Tousey. He still sat with his head back against the rafters, every now and then sniffing the air reminiscently, sometimes made restless, sometimes apparently soothed, by whatever past he was living over, and so absorbed that he scarcely roused when at last, with a sound of iron clinking on iron, the same register which he had opened and lifted out began to rise slowly from its setting and fell to one side on the floor. From the vacant hole, like a jack-in-the-box from its hiding-place, rose up Mrs. Joseph's head, her eyes searching the attic, her brow a little anxious, and her face flushed as only a cooking-stove can flush the human countenance. There was but room for her head to emerge. By an effort she added one hand, and a head is all one actually needs in conversation, while one hand can lend enough freedom of gesture to accompany speech. Her voice was that of a tired woman, none the less it rang with cheerful determination.

"Uncle Elijah," said Mrs. Joseph, quickly, "I hope you're not tired of waiting for your Christmas dinner. You haven't any chair, have you? I wish I could push one up through this hole, but it won't go. If you'll pull that trunk you're sitting on close to the register, it'll be almost like sitting at the table with us. I've put your plate right under the hole, and I'm going to fill it and hand your Christmas dinner up to you by way of this step-ladder

I'm standing on. I'll hand up the soup first."

Mrs. Joseph's head vanished before Mr. Tousey could reply, and up through the hole thus left open came a direct whiff of soup that brought him trembling to his feet. He had been fasting since that frugal early breakfast of bread and bacon, but it was not hunger that drew his faltering feet irresistibly to the edge of the register. He told himself, as he dragged the pig-skin trunk along with him, that even for the few moments he must spend by that opening he was too old, too tired, and too agitated to stand; but once seated on the trunk and again peering down the open hole, astonishment held him motionless. On the table before him were rich moulded jellies and richer cakes, icings as smooth as glass, and whipped syllabubs that stood alone, all as visions of what had been and was now no more; while slowly obscuring the remoter view, up the ladder, approaching him nearer and nearer, came Annie with a plate of soup in her hand. From that plate steamed an odor that only the gumbo soup made by one hand had ever given off, and in the plate itself, along with the delightful little vegetable bits that belong in all gumbo soups, swam crisp little batter-balls that Madam Tousey, and only

"NEARER CAME ANNIE, WITH A PLATE OF SOUP IN HER HAND."

Madam Tousey, had ever known how to create. Before Mr. Tousey could recover breath enough to speak, Mrs. Joseph had flung the napkin she was carrying over her shoulder across her uncle's knees, and set the soup carefully on the pig-skin trunk beside him. She laid in it the tempting silver spoon, and then she disappeared as quickly as she had come. Mr. Tousey was alone in the attic with the gumbo soup. Under his very nose stood the mess of pottage, steaming, beckoning, reeking with invitation. The result, so far as Mr. Tousey was concerned, was purely mechanical. He was a man in a dream. Up the ladder, following the soup, trooped oysters fried in bacon blankets, turkey that he knew had been stuffed with a dressing which was also Madam Tousey's precious secret. Still, as in a dream, Mr. Tousey ate on and on. With misty eyes he saw the plates coming and going, resting upon his knees for too short delectable moments, then disappearing, only to be replaced by others as bewildering. The sound of pleasant voices and laughter and family chatter came to him from below. He had room for but three sensations—astonishment, taste, and a kind of dismay. Every dish, from soup to salad, was prepared in some fashion that differed from the ordinary, but in every case Mr.

Tousey recognized the difference as a lover rec-
ognizes a long-lost love.

When the ice-cream came at last, his spoon
hovered above it in a hand that trembled.
Would it — could it be possible that it might
contain in its flavoring that subtle, nutty,
spirituous, defined, yet indescribable tastiness
that had made Madam Tousey's cream famous through all the county? Mr. Tousey
raised the spoon slowly to his mouth. It
did !

"Uncle Elijah," said Mrs. Joseph, making
one of her sudden appearances through the
register, "I don't know why in the world I
haven't thought of it before. It's just this
moment come to me how to get you out with a
turn of the hand. I'm going to hand you up a
block and tackle, and you can tie the block to
that rafter over the cupboard and pass the end
of the rope down here through the register,
then we'll all hang on it and pull the cupboard
right up into the ceiling and let you out. Here's
your coffee, sir, and just as soon as you've drunk
that, unless you'd like more ice - cream first—
Why, Uncle Elijah !"

Mr. Tousey was wiping tears of emotion
from his eyes with his large red silk handkerchief.

"It's nothing," he said, recovering, and looking down appealingly into Annie's face ; "only I don't care about being gotten out of here, Annie Tousey. I don't care at all. I'd just as lief stay forever right here on this pig-skin trunk and have you pass things up to me. Honey, you say you've got a little more of that ice-cream ?"

Mrs. Joseph's face disappeared instantly, but in a moment rose again into sight — radiant, yet subdued, as a full harvest moon rises and shines on a gathered harvest.

"Uncle Elijah," she said, wooingly, "you can have the cream if you want, but here's some pie I think you'll like better. It's a deep family pie, the kind grandmother used to make. If you like this one, I'll promise you to have this kind of ice-cream for our dinner every summer Sunday, and the family pie for dinner every winter Sunday, or anything else you may happen to fancy." Her manner grew fairly portentous in its significance as she paused for his reply. "These are to be no pie-crust promises, Uncle Elijah, I assure you. If I promise, it shall be exactly as I say."

Mr. Tousey understood. He looked at Annie, and he looked at the pie. It was three inches deep. It had the bosom of a swan, with just that melting tint of brown that marks the perfect pie.

"Annie," said Uncle Elijah, solemnly, "it shall be exactly as you say." And he held out his hand for the pie.

AN I. O. U.

Dramatis Personæ: MR. ATWOOD and ALINE, his ward.
Time: A 1st of April. Morning.

ACT I

*The curtain rises on a lawyer's office, the walls
lined with sad-colored books, the shelves tipped
with dark green leather and brass-headed
nails, once bright, but now succumbing to the
prevailing neutral tint. The heavy mahogany
chairs are covered with the same dark leather.
The green felt top of the desk at which* MR.
ATWOOD *is discovered sitting is black where
the ink spots are new, rusty where they are
old, and half covered by papers and pamphlets.
The April sunshine streams in through an
open window at the left of the desk, and falls
on a deep chair placed there. A door at the
back of the room opens softly.*

(Enter ALINE, *dressed as a school-girl. She
moves timidly across the floor, and pauses before the desk.)*

III

Madame Armand say when she knows that you have run away from her to your stern guardian?

Aline. You are not stern.

Mr. Atwood. Ah, you do not know me. I am going to be very stern now.

Aline (*with a quick glance*). You couldn't. (*She smiles.*)

Mr. Atwood (*smiling also, and shaking his head*). No, I'm afraid you are right. But you have not yet told me what Madame Armand is going to say to this escapade?

Aline. Nothing — she won't know. I slipped away so cleverly.

Mr. Atwood (*cautiously*). Then you did not mean to run away forever?

Aline (*laughing*). Oh no; did you think so? I only wanted to see you quite alone. I had something to say to you.

Mr. Atwood (*with a breath of relief*). Ah! Shall you be afraid when you go back to Madame Armand, if she should find you out, Aline?

Aline. No-o. But she won't.

Mr. Atwood. I am afraid we shall have to take her into our confidence, my child.

Aline. You are not going to tell her of me?

Mr. Atwood. I am going to take you back

to her myself. But she shall say nothing to you. I promise you that. I will come to the school to-night, and you shall then see me entirely alone, and tell me all you want; but I must take you back to Madame Armand—and at once, Aline!

Aline. You are going to drive me away?

Mr. Atwood. I am going to drive you away in a carriage, with myself on the seat beside you, that's all.

Aline (*passionately withdrawing from him*). If you send me away now, I will never come back to you. I am not a baby. I won't be taken home by my hand, and have my nurse told not to scold me. I am going back alone. (*As she reaches the door* Mr. Atwood *follows and detains her.*)

Mr. Atwood (*gravely*). Stay, Aline. I will listen now, my dear. (*She resists for a moment, but is conquered by a flood of excited tears.* Mr. Atwood *leads her to the arm-chair by the window.*)

Mr. Atwood. Sit here and rest, first.

Aline (*rubbing her eyes with her hands childishly.*) May I take off my h-hat?

Mr. Atwood. Of course you may. See, here is my chair close by yours, and here am I in it. Now, what is it? (*He unties her hat ribbons, lays the hat on the floor, and sits in a chair near* ALINE.)

Aline (*still brokenly*). I want to know what you are going to do with me?

Mr. Atwood. Do with you?

Aline. Yes; you are not going to do what Madame Armand says, are you?

Mr. Atwood. What does she say?

Aline (*indignantly*). That I am to spend next winter with her, and that she is to take me out into what she calls "de vorld"—and that you said so.

Mr. Atwood (*frowning slightly*). Madame Armand should have let me tell you my plans. Why do you object, Aline?

Aline. Then you did say it.

Mr. Atwood. Madame Armand knows the world, and could show it to you very well and pleasantly. She has done so with many other girls. And you like her, do you not? I thought so.

Aline. I have not minded learning from her, but is that to be my home?

Mr. Atwood. It has been your home for many years. You called it that just now yourself.

Aline. She can't even say home in her language. That's not a home. It's only the place I live.

116

Mr. Atwood. Doesn't that mean home ?

Aline (*reproachfully*). You know it does not.

Mr. Atwood (*smiling*). No, not always, I admit. I have no home myself, you know, outside of my club. But I thought you were happy with Madame Armand.

Aline. I was quite willing to go to school to her, but next year will be different. I shall be a woman then, and I did not think I should have to wait longer than that.

Mr. Atwood (*perplexed*). For what ?

Aline. To live with you.

Mr. Atwood. With me, my dear !

Aline. If I had known only Madame Armand, it would have satisfied me, I suppose, but I was seeing you always, and always looking forward to our living together. You surely remember our plans ?

Mr. Atwood (*after a moment's silence*). Tell me them over again, Aline.

Aline (*surprised*). Why, you used to be saying it over and over again whenever you came to see me. You used to say we should live together in a little house, and that you would never marry, and I should keep the house for you. Surely you have not forgotten !

Mr. Atwood. When and where did we last speak of that ?

Aline. In the garden at Madame's summer home. You were sitting on a bench, and you lifted me on your knee, and we even decided on our furniture.

Mr. Atwood (*rising, and looking out of the window, his back to* ALINE). And you never remember my saying this after you grew too old to be perched on my knee? .

Aline. No, but I never forgot it. That has always been *home* to me. Why don't you speak to me? I believe you don't want me.

Mr. Atwood (*turning quickly*). Dear child, you must never think that. (*He rests his hand on the back of her chair, looking down at her.*) How can I make you understand? You know about as much of the world as the roar of life out there in the street might tell you, and that is all.

Aline (*eagerly*). You could teach it to me— and far better than Madame Armand.

Mr. Atwood. No; here I have only a tiny corner of life to show you, and see how I stammer and stutter over it. (*He sits again by* ALINE, *and covers her hands, which lie in her lap, with his own.*) Tell me, my dear, did you ever see just such a household as you describe? Did you ever hear or read of one? Run over your schoolmates' lives— what became of them as they went out from the school?

Aline (*sadly*). That is not the same thing. They all had a father or a mother to go to, or at least an uncle or an aunt. I have never had any one but you, and now I do think you don't want me. (*She tries to withdraw her hands.* MR. ATWOOD *holds them fast.*)

Mr. Atwood (*earnestly*). Aline, I do want you. What could give me greater happiness than to keep you with me always, and have you care for me, and I for you? I have no home either, you know. Do you suppose I am never lonely? Remember all that, and then realize how hard it must be for me to say no.

Aline (*tearfully*). Then what makes you say it?

Mr. Atwood (*very gently*). Think a moment, dear child. I am an old man to you, but the world still calls me young; and you are a child to me, but the world would call you a woman. We are too young and too old, and we cannot possibly stretch out the years between us, try as we might. Do you understand now? Look about your own small world, and you will see that kind of household only belonging to married people.

Aline (*sobbing*). Then why don't you marry me?

Mr. Atwood (*dropping* ALINE's *hands and rising hastily*). My dear child (*he continues with effort*), I must have done very wrongly, but it was without intention to deceive or play on your feelings. I drew a pathetic picture of a homeless life which does not exist, and of a loneliness which is not mine. I am neither lonely nor unhappy. I am not even uncomfortable, and you must not feel sorry for me, Aline. (ALINE *sobs on, and* MR. ATWOOD *continues, entreatingly.*) Suppose I were to marry you, my dear. Can't you see that I should be doing a very wicked thing?

Aline (*brushing away her tears*). No, you would not be wicked. If you knew how I hated the thought of being with Madame Armand, you wouldn't say so.

Mr. Atwood (*his expression relaxing suddenly into relief and amusement*). Child, what an unnecessary scare you gave me. Come, dry your eyes, and we will talk it all over. What a watery little woman it is! See how you have tear-stained your white glove. It is quite wet. Let me pull it off for you. (*He sits down again and draws her glove from her hand, finger by finger.*) Now we will talk this all out comfortably, and leave nothing to think of afterwards. Did you suppose I could be tempted into rob-bing baby-carriages? And what a baby you are, Aline!

Aline (*with dignity*). I shall be eighteen very soon.

Mr. Atwood. And I shall be two-score in a few years. How would you like being hampered with a gray-haired husband then?

Aline. I should like it dearly.

Mr. Atwood (*hastily*). You don't know what you would like when you are a woman. Do you know what even my best friends would say? That I had kept a little heiress in a pill-box, and married her before she had a chance to peep out; and it would be quite true.

Aline (*impatiently*). If having money is only to make me unhappy, I shall give it all to Madame Armand the day I come of age.

Mr. Atwood (*gravely*). Even then, my child, it would not be honorable for me to marry you.

Aline (*reproachfully*). And you care more for that than for me?

Mr. Atwood. No; you have been as my own child for so many years, that I am afraid, if your happiness and my honor were put in the scales, my honor would kick the beam. But it is your happiness that I am considering now; for I could not make you happy, try as I might.

Aline. Why not?

Mr. Atwood (*decidedly*). Because you do not love me.

Aline. I do love you.

Mr. Atwood. No, you do not, or you would be less sure of it, and you would not tell me so. You are fond of me, as I am of you, but you do not love me, my dear.

Aline. What is the difference?

Mr. Atwood (*smiling*). You will know some day, and then I will let you marry him.

Aline. How shall I know?

Mr. Atwood. Ah, that was just the order of question I wanted to leave Madame Armand to answer.

Aline. No; tell me yourself.

Mr. Atwood. Well, first of all, you will know without asking, and deny it, even to yourself. You will stand in the shadow of a needle, and fancy yourself concealed. You will be troubled when with him, and miserable when away from him. And then I will give you to him, and not before.

Aline. But I am miserable at the thought of being away from you.

Mr. Atwood. You are miserable at the thought of being with Madame Armand. Tell me the truth, Aline; do you ever miss me after I leave you?

Aline. Indeed I do.

Mr. Atwood. How much, and for how long?

Aline (*thoughtfully*). I don't have much time between lessons, but I want you to come back soon, and I always cry until the class-bell rings after you go. (MR. ATWOOD *stoops and kisses her hand with exaggerated gallantry.*)

Mr. Atwood. That is good of you, Aline; you miss me more than I thought, my dear. But some day, although your eyes may cry less, your heart will cry more. You won't want him back *soon*, but at once and forever. And no lesson-books nor class-bells on earth will be able to make you forget. Then you will remember your old guardian's words, and laugh at the idea of loving him.

Aline. No; for indeed I do love you.

Mr. Atwood (*tenderly*). I know you do, and I love you dearly, my child. We are not ashamed to confess our loves, are we? There lies the defect.

Aline. You don't love me, or you wouldn't let me be so unhappy.

Mr. Atwood. You are not to be unhappy.

Aline. I shall be unhappy with Madame Armand.

Mr. Atwood. You are not to be left with Madame Armand.

AN I. O. U.

Aline (*radiantly*). You mean to keep me yourself, after all ?

Mr. Atwood. Practically, since you are foolish enough to want me. I don't see it all quite clearly yet, but do you think you would like to live with my sister ?

Aline. With your sister ? I thought you said——

Mr. Atwood. I will take a house for you both near my own rooms. She is a widow, you know, and, being quite as mistaken as yourself regarding me, will do all I wish. You will see me every day, and oftener, perhaps. That will be your own home, and my second home. Will that satisfy you ?

Aline (*starting to her feet*). You are in earnest ?

Mr. Atwood (*rising also*). In dead earnest.

Aline. I can't, no, I can't believe it !

Mr. Atwood (*laughing*). Shut your eyes and try hard, and, whatever you do, don't cry again. You have been a naughty child, and gained all you cried for. Now be good, and thank me prettily. (ALINE, *with a cry of delight, clasps her hands on his arm and lifts her face, offering him her lips.* MR. ATWOOD *looks at her and hesitates. He lays his finger lightly on her lips.*) No ; we will keep those for the lover to come.

AN I. O. U.

You are pleased, then? You want nothing
more? Think, now, while I am in the melting
mood.

Aline (*knitting her brows with difficulty*). I
don't think of anything more that I could
want.

Mr. Atwood (*quizzically*). Not even me?

Aline. You said I should see you.

Mr. Atwood. And you don't want to marry
me now?

Aline (*shyly*). I do, if you want me to. You
have been so good.

Mr. Atwood. Aline, confess the truth. Now
that you have escaped Madame Armand, you
want to throw me over. You never loved me
at all.

Aline. It was you who said that. I told you
I did.

Mr. Atwood. In the past tense already, I
vow! *Do* you?

Aline (*hanging her head*). If all that you told
me just now is true, then perhaps I don't.

Mr. Atwood (*laughing aloud*). Very well,
then, I shall never ask you to marry me again.
I have been refused by a chit of seventeen, on
this first day of April.

Aline (*looking at him thoughtfully*). You
have been so good to me. Will you take me

home now ? (*She moves apart from him, and speaks softly, lowering her eyes.*) I shall love you forever for what you did then. But all the same—

Mr. Atwood (*looks at her keenly. Aside*). Have I said too much ? (*Aloud.*) Here is your hat, Aline. (*He lifts her hat from the floor and watches her tie it on.* ALINE *avoids his eyes. They move to the door, which* MR. ATWOOD *opens. As he stands aside for her to pass out,* ALINE *glances back over her shoulder.*)

Aline (*mischievously*). You must never tell any one that I offered myself to you, you know.

Mr. Atwood (*following her*). Aline !

CURTAIN

ACT II

Scene : The same.

Time : One year later.

Curtain rises on MR. ATWOOD *seated at his desk, looking at the calendar he holds in his hand. The date marked is April 1st. He lays down the calendar thoughtfully, draws his paper towards him, dips his pen in the ink, and begins to write. The door at the back of the room opens softly.*

(*Enter* ALINE, *dressed in walking-costume. She crosses the floor on tiptoe, and stands laughing at the other side of the desk.*)

Aline. How angry are you this time? (*As* MR. ATWOOD *looks up and attempts to rise, she motions him back.*) Don't move; I am coming to you. (*She walks around the desk and sinks in a chair by his side, still laughing, and holding out her hand.*) You have not bade me good-morning yet.

Mr. Atwood (*holding the hand she offers*). Aline, you are incorrigible. How did you get here this time?

Aline. In the same way—a cab. Now, why don't you scold?

Mr. Atwood. Because I cannot, and you know it. This is a flagrant abuse of power. Is my sister in town?

Aline. Oh no, she is at the sea-side, where you left her.

Mr. Atwood (*reproachfully*). And where I left you.

Aline. I know; I have run away again. I took the early train this morning. I wanted to see you.

AN I. O. U.

Mr. Atwood. I should be more than human to scold now. That was cleverly done, Aline. What do you want? Experience, alas, has taught you that you have only to ask.

Aline. I wanted to see you—

Mr. Atwood. You saw me three days ago.

Aline. I wanted to see you again. Are you busy?

Mr. Atwood. No; as usual, I am at your disposal.

Aline. You were writing when I came in.

Mr. Atwood. Did you expect to find me kicking my heels? No; to tell the truth, if a penny postage-stamp had been put on my thoughts, I am afraid you would have received them.

Aline (*opening her purse laughingly, selects a coin, which she lays on the table*). A penny for your thoughts, then, as you have put your price on them.

Mr. Atwood (*taking possession of the coin, and laughing also*). I will give you an I. O. U. See here. (*He takes up his pen and writes rapidly.* ALINE *looks over his shoulder.*)

Mr. Atwood (*reads*). "I. O. U. my thoughts, to be delivered in ripe season." Does that answer? (ALINE *takes the paper, folds it, and lays it away in her reticule with mock carefulness.*)

128

Mr. Atwood (*watching her*). And now, what? I am not vain enough to believe that you only wanted to see me. Let me think. You were afraid I would buy your new dining-room table without you, after all. Is that it?

Aline. I told you I didn't care about selecting it.

Mr. Atwood. And I told you I would not buy it without you. I am a creature of habit. The old table is just right. Suppose your new table proved too wide for you to hand my coffee-cup across yourself? I should never dine with you again, if you invited me every night. You must go with me and test it.

Aline. Indeed I shall not. What would the cabinet-maker think?

Mr. Atwood. He would think me an old fool, I imagine, and (*pausing and looking at* ALINE) I fear he would be quite right. I must content myself with taking him the measurement, I suppose. But come, Aline, I want you to sit over there in the arm-chair by the window, where you sat the first time you came here, one year ago to-day. I have held it sacred to you since then. (*He leads* ALINE *to the arm-chair, and sits near her.*) I sat just here, opposite to you, did I not? But then you were my obedient ward—and to-day I am your obedient guardian.

AN I. O. U.

Aline (*lifting her hat from her head and laying it on her knee*). You have not told me that I might take off my hat yet, and you did the time before. (*She passes her hands over her hair.*)

Mr. Atwood (*smiling*). Mark the year's difference! Then you humbly asked my permission. To-day you don't wait for it. Time flies, but we fly also. Are you satisfied with the changes of your year, Aline?

Aline (*using the crown of her hat as a cushion for her bonnet-pins, thrusting them in and out as she talks*). Yes, I am satisfied; but your sister is not satisfied for me.

Mr. Atwood. What displeases her?

Aline. That I am not married.

Mr. Atwood (*quickly*). Did she say that to you?

Aline. Not that exactly, but I know how anxious she is to see me settled. She thinks I am in danger of throwing myself away, you know.

Mr. Atwood. Why?

Aline (*indifferently*). Oh, because I am wealthy, and because I am pretty.

Mr. Atwood (*laughing*). You know that you are wealthy, because I could not well keep that from you. But how do you know you are pretty?

AN I. O. U.

Aline (*demurely*). I have been told so.

Mr. Atwood. I never told you so.

Aline (*looking up at him and raising her eyebrows*). You are telling me so now.

Mr. Atwood. What kind of discipline does this show? You ought to stand in awe of me, Aline.

Aline. I do sometimes. I was horribly afraid of you the night before we left home. I was afraid you would be angry, as your sister was.

Mr. Atwood. Was she angry with you—and why?

Aline (*thrusting the pins into her hat and looking down*). Because I *couldn't* do what she wanted me to—you remember. I was afraid to tell you I had sent him away, because I knew you wanted it so much, too; but, indeed, I had tried my very best.

Mr. Atwood (*leaning towards her*). And you thought I should be angry! that I wanted you to marry!

Aline. But you did, did you not? You kept asking him here and there, and making me go to places with him when I didn't want to.

Mr. Atwood. No, I did not want you to marry him. When you told me you could not, I was indecently happy to hear it.

131

Aline. Then why did you feel one way and act another? Of course I misunderstood you.

Mr. Atwood. Can you see no reason?

Aline. I call it very unreasonable.

Mr. Atwood (*earnestly*). No, he had everything to offer you—strength of body and mind, a real devotion, I think, wealth, position—and youth. I determined he should have every chance, but as for wishing it—no, Aline. (*He rises and moves to the desk, where he unlocks a drawer and takes from it a long white glove, which he hands* ALINE.) You left it here in your last visit. Do you remember?

Aline (*puzzled, and turning the glove over*). No — why, yes, I do remember. I searched everywhere for it afterwards, and finally threw away the mate. Why didn't you give me this before?

Mr. Atwood. I have not given it to you now.

Aline (*turning the glove over again; laughs*). It may not be wasted, after all, as it happens to be a right-hand glove. This will do for my wedding-day. Keep it for me. When I want it I will ask you for it. (MR. ATWOOD *takes the glove from her and puts it in his pocket silently.*)

Aline (*laughing*). How seriously you take it!

Mr. Atwood. I am thinking of the confession

I have to make to you. I was going down to the sea-side to see you this afternoon.

Aline. But you wrote that you were very busy, and that you couldn't possibly come.

Mr. Atwood. And it was quite true.

Aline. Then how could you?

Mr. Atwood. I couldn't from that point of view, but I was coming. I wanted to see you.

Aline (mischievously). You saw me three days ago. That was your reply to me.

Mr. Atwood. I wanted to see you again. That was your answer.

Aline. Then you do miss me a little?

Mr. Atwood (smiling). A little.

Aline. Only a little?

Mr. Atwood (taking her two hands in his and raising them to his lips). I have not paid you that homage since the day when you last sat in this chair. You say that you have wanted me, Aline. Multiply that tenfold, and you will know how I was wanting you. I told you I was a creature of habit. When you left town, I turned back again to my old lines of life, and it was as if they had never fitted me. I had drifted from them, and in revenge they would not have me again. My old haunts were but places revisited. Do you know what I mean? What am I to do? I was coming to ask you.

Aline (touching the reticule at her side). Was that the thought you sold me?

Mr. Atwood. That and something further. Will you present your paper now, Aline? I am more than ready to tell my thought.

Aline. Let *me* tell something first. I was not quite honest when I said I came for nothing. (*She turns her face from him as she continues, speaking softly.*) Last year, when I sat in this chair, you told me that if I really cared, I would be so unhappy in a separation that nothing could make me forget—

Mr. Atwood (eagerly). Yes?

Aline (her face still averted). And that I then would learn the difference between—just being fond of some one and something else.

Mr. Atwood (bending nearer, and half circling her with his arm). Go on, Aline.

Aline. And that when my eyes cried less than my heart, I would understand.

Mr. Atwood. And now, dear?

Aline (turning to him suddenly and hiding her face against his arm). You told me that if I cared really I couldn't say it, and I don't think I can say it at all.

Mr. Atwood. Then let me say it for you, Aline.

Aline. That was what I came for. When we

134

were separated, then I knew, as you said I would— Will you bring him back to me? (MR. ATWOOD *bends over her in silence. As* ALINE *attempts to rise he gently prevents her by laying his hand on her head. Once his lips touch her hair, and then he releases her and stands beside her.* ALINE, *rising also, glances up at him eagerly. As she clasps her hands appealingly on his arm, he looks down at her.*)

Mr. Atwood (*slowly*). Yes, I will bring him back to you.

Aline (*anxiously*). You are not vexed with me?

Mr. Atwood. No, my child.

Aline. And you will still love me?

Mr. Atwood. Always, Aline. (*As she still clings to him he rouses with effort.*) All is as it should be; I shall do my part. I will give you to him as I promised, and dance at your wedding, dear. Are you satisfied?

Aline. How good you are to me. (*She lifts her face, offering him her lips.*)

Mr. Atwood (*framing her face in his hands*). No, those are not for me, Aline. (*As he releases her and turns away, a rap at the door calls him.* MR. ATWOOD *crosses the room and opens the door to receive a card which is handed in to him. He reads it and then looks at* ALINE. *Re-*

turning to her side, he speaks steadily.) Aline,
some one is waiting to see me in the outer office—some one who can offer you a great deal,
my dear—an honorable name, an eager devotion, and the pride of strength and youth.   He
asks me if I can spare him a few moments.
What shall I tell him, dear ?   Shall I say that
I will spare him far more than that—and that
it is waiting for him here ?   (*He takes her glove
from his pocket, and holds it towards her.*) Take
your glove if that is to be my answer. (*As*
Aline, *with bowed head, holds out her hand,* Mr.
Atwood *lays the white glove across her palm,
and, gently opening her reticule, draws out the
written form. As he passes the open window on
his way from the room, he pauses to tear the
paper into fragments, fluttering the white scraps
out into the air.*)

CURTAIN

A WILL AND A WAY

It was in that pleasant season of the year when there is a ladder at every apple-tree, and every man met on the road is driving with his left hand and eating a red apple from his right. At this season, as regularly as the year rolled round, old Carshena Hubblestone nearly died of cramps, caused by gorging himself with the apples falling almost into his mouth from the spreading boughs of fruit trees that fairly roofed his low - built house. This was, as it were, Carshena's one dissipation. The apples cost him nothing, and his medical attention after his bouts cost him nothing either, for he was the son of a physician, and though his father was long since dead, the village doctor would not render a bill.

"Crow don't eat crow," Dr. Michel answered, roughly, when Carshena weakly asked him what he owed. The chance of thus roistering so cheaply is not presented to every man, and reluctance to let such a bargain pass was per-

137

haps what helped to lend periodicity to the old man's attacks. Dr. Michel always held that this was his chief incentive, and, be this as it might, it was very certain that apples and bargains were the only two things on earth for which Carshena was ever known to show a weakness, creditable or discreditable. Most small communities have their rich men and their mean men, but in the village of Leonard the two were one.

As the years passed on and Carshena's head whitened, it naturally grew to be a less and less easy task for Dr. Michel to bring his patient back to the place where he had been before apples ripened. If the situation had not tickled a spice of humor that lay under the physician's grim exterior he would have refused these autumnal attentions. As it was he confined himself to futile warnings and threats of non-attendance, but he always did obey the summons when it came. The townsfolk of Leonard would all have taken the same humorous view of this weakness of Carshena's but for the trouble which it gave his too-good sister Adelia —liked and pitied by every one. Adelia nursed her brother in each attack with a tenderness and anxiety that aggravated all the community. Nobody but his sister Adelia was ever anxious over Carshena. It was therefore like a bolt from a clear sky when, in this chronicled autumn, the following conversation took place at the Hubblestones' gate. Dr. Michel's buggy was wheeling out to the main road as Mr. Gowan, the town butcher, was about to drive through the gateway.

"Well, doctor," called the genial man of blood, a broad grin on his round face, "how's the patient?"

"He's gone, sir," said Dr. Michel, drawing rein. The butcher drew up his horse sharply, his ruddy face changing so suddenly that the doctor laughed outright.

"Gone!" echoed Mr. Gowan. "Not gone?"

"Yes, sir, as I warned him time and again he would go."

The butcher shook his head and pursed his lips, the news slowly penetrating his mind. "Well, I certainly would hate to die of eatin' apples," he said at last.

"I guess you'll find you hate to die of any-thing, when the time comes," said the more ex-perienced physician. "Carshena," he added, "got nothing he didn't bring on himself, if that's any comfort to him."

"Don't speak hard of the dead, doctor," urged Mr. Gowan. "We've all got to follow him some day. He wasn't a nice man in some ways, Carshena wasn't, but—"

"He was a nasty old man in most ways," snapped the doctor.

"Don't say such things now, doctor, don't," urged the good butcher. "'Ain't he paid in his full price, whatever his sins was? Poor soul! he can't be worse 'n dead."

"Oh yes, he can, and for one I believe he is," interrupted the doctor. His crisp white hair seemed to Mr. Gowan to curl tighter over his head as he frowned with some thought he was nursing. "You haven't seen the will I had to witness this morning!" he burst out. "Just you wait a little! Upon my soul! the more I think of it the madder I get! It's out of my bailiwick, but if I were a lawyer I'd walk right up now under those old apple-trees yonder, and before that man was cold on his bed I'd have his sister's promise to break his old will into a thousand splinters! Wait till you hear it. Good-morning."

When the will was read and its contents announced, the town of Leonard, including its butcher, took the doctor's view to a man.

"A brute," said Dr. Michel, hotly, "who has let his old sister work her hands to the bone for him, and then turned her off like some old worn-out horse, has, in my opinion, no right to a will at all. How about setting this will aside in his sister's interests, judge?"

A little convocation of the leading spirits of Leonard were met together in Dr. Michel's office to discuss the matter of Carshena's will, and what should be done with Adelia, cast on the charity of the village. Judge Bowles, when appealed to, raised his mild blue eyes and looked around the company.

"Adelia," he said, " is the best sister I ever knew. Had the man no shame?"

"Shame!" said the town's barber, with a reminiscent chuckle; " why, he came into my parlors one day and asked me if I'd cut the back of his hair for twelve cents, and let him cut the front himself; and I did it, for the joke of the thing! He saved thirteen cents that way."

"Gentlemen, gentlemen!" demurred the judge; but amid the general laughter the tax-gatherer's voice rose:

" There isn't a tax he didn't fight. This town got nothing out of Carshena Hubblestone that he could help paying; and now he leaves us his relatives to support."

Judge Bowles rose to his feet.

"Gentlemen," he said, in mild but earnest

rebuke, "the man is dead. We all know what his character was without these distressing particulars. It is entirely true that we owe him nothing, but a dead man is defenceless, and his will is his will, and law is law. Did you ever think what a solemn title a man's last will is? It means just what it says, gentlemen—his last will, his last wish and power of disposition writ down on paper, concerning his own property. It's a solemn thing to break that."

"A man's no business having such a will and a disposition to write down on paper," said the doctor. "What are the exact terms of the will, judge?"

"Very simple," said Judge Bowles, dryly. "The whole estate is to be sold, and the entire proceeds, every cent realized, except what is kept back for repairs and care, is to be applied to the purchase of a suitable lot and the raising of a great monument over the mortal remains of Carshena Hubblestone."

"While his sister starves!" added Dr. Michel.

"Gee!" exclaimed the kindly butcher. He had heard all this before, but thus repeated it seemed to strike him anew, as somehow it did all the rest of the company. They sat looking at each other in silence, with indrawings of the breath and compression of lips.

"There is this extenuating circumstance," said the doctor, with dangerous smoothness: "our lamented brother was aware that unless he erected a monument to himself he might never enjoy one. We—the judge, Mr. Gowan, and myself—are made sole executors under the will—without pay. In Carshena's life Adelia was his white slave. In his death, doubtless, he felt he could trust her to make no protest. I wish you could have seen her with him as I have, gentlemen. I shall call it a shame upon us if we let her eat the bitter bread of our charity. She's been put upon and trodden down, but she's still a proud woman in her way, and we've got to save her from a bitter old age. We've got to do it."

"It's the kind of thing that discourages one's belief in humanity," said the judge, in a lowered tone. "This affair might be only absurd if it weren't for the sister's share in it. As it is, it's a revelation of human selfishness that makes one heart-sick."

Dr. Michel's laugh rang out irreverently.

"It's perfectly absurd, sister or no sister," he said. "Nobody, not one of us, loved Carshena in life—though I think now we didn't hate him half enough—and here in death he's fixed it so the town's got to pay for his responsibilities

while his money builds him a grand monument, and he don't deserve a foot-stone! I
call that about as absurd as you'll get anywhere. I'll grant you it makes me downright
sick at my stomach, judge, but it don't touch
my heart. No, sir. Keep your organs separate,
as I do, gentlemen. There's one thing certain"
—he drew the eyes of his audience with uplifted finger—"if we can't outwit this will somehow, we'll be the laughing-stock of this whole
county. I don't care a snap of my finger if
Carshena has a monument as high as Haman's
gallows, if only his sister is protected at the
same time."

"Well, short of breaking the will, what would
you suggest, doctor?" asked Judge Bowles, with
a slight stiffness. He had not liked the familiar discourse on his organs, but the doctor did
not care. The judge was ruffled at last, which
was exactly what he desired.

"Suggest?" he cried, laughing. "I don't
know; but I know there never was a will
written that couldn't be driven through with
a coach and six if the right man sits on the
box. You're the lawyer, judge."

The judge was a lawyer, as he then and there
proceeded to prove. He rose to his feet and
spoke in his old-fashioned style:

A WILL AND A WAY

"Gentlemen, I think I speak for this company when I say that we would strongly object to the breaking of this will as a bad precedent in the community. We wish it carried out to the very letter. Our fellow-townsman knew his sister's needs better than we, and he chose to leave her needy. There are many, many things this town sorely wants, as he also knew, but he chose to use his money otherwise. What a monument to him it would have been had he built us the new school-house our town requires! The wet south lot down by the old mill is an eyesore to the village. Had he used that land and drained it and set up a school-house there, or indeed any public building, what a different meeting this would have been! He was our only man of wealth, and he leaves not so much as a town-clock to thank him for. No; a monument to *himself* is what his will calls for, and a monument he shall have. If we failed him here, which of us would feel sure that our own wills would be carried out? In the confidence of these four walls we can say that the difficulties of the inscription and the style of monument seem insuperable. I know but one man to whom I would intrust this delicate commission. I feel confident that he would not render us absurd by too conspicuous a monument or too

K   145

florid an inscription. Need I name Dr. Michel?"

"Out of my bailiwick," cried the doctor—
"'way out of my bailiwick." But his voice was drowned in the confusion of the popular acclaim that was forming him into a committee of one. The kindly butcher made his way to the doctor's side under cover of the noise.

"Take it, doctor; now do take it," he whispered in his ear. "There ain't a man in the town that can shave this pig if you can't. I was sayin' just yesterday you're lost in this little place of ourn. You've got more sense than's often called for here. Here's the chance for you to show 'em what you can do. Do take it."

The physician looked at the wheedling little butcher with a glance from his blue eye that was half kindly, half irritated. "Well, I'll take it," he cried; "I'll take it; and I thank you for your confidence, gentlemen."

It was a full month before the little company met again in the doctor's office, but during that period they knew Dr. Michel had not been idle in the matter intrusted to his care. He was seen in earnest consultation with the town's first masons, the best carpenters, the local architect; and these worthies, under close and eager examination, gave answers that dashed the un-

A WILL AND A WAY

spoken hopes of those who questioned. Here
were *bona fide* bids asked for on so much ma-
sonry, so much carpentering, and the architect
had been ordered to send in designs of monu-
ments, how high he deemed it unprofessional
to state ; but arguing inversely, they judged
by the length of his countenance that the
measurements were not short—he had particularly hated Carshena. It was, for all these
reasons, a rather anxious-looking company that
met in Dr. Michel's office at his summons, and
the doctor's own face was not reassuring as he
opened the meeting.

"Well, gentlemen," he said, slowly, "it's a
thankless task you've given me, but such as it
is, I hope you will find I have performed it to
your satisfaction. Here are various plans for
the monument to be erected to our late fellow-
citizen, and here is a plan of the ground that
it has seemed to me most suitable to purchase.
It has been a task peculiarly uncongenial to
me, because I, I suppose, know more than any
of you here how this money is needed where it
ought to have gone. I saw Adelia yesterday,
and lonely and ghost-ridden as that old house
would be to any of us, it's a home to her that's
to be sold over her head to build this." He
laid his hand on the papers he had thrown

147

down on the table before him. The little company looked silently at each other, with faces as downcast as if they were to blame. It was Judge Bowles who spoke first.

"Gentlemen," he said, "we must not let ourselves feel too responsible in this matter. We are only following our plain duty. Show us the monument which you consider best, doctor."

The doctor was silently turning over the papers. "Family feeling is a queer thing," he said, meditatively. "When I saw Adelia, I asked her if she wanted a neighbor to sleep in the house at night.

"'There's nothing here for robbers to take, Dr. Michel,' she said; 'and if it's ghosts you think I'm afraid of, I only wish from my heart ghosts would come back to visit me. Everybody of my blood is dead.'"

"It's very pitiful," said Judge Bowles, slowly.

The doctor turned on him instantly. "Do you seem to feel now that you could countenance breaking the will, judge?"

"No," said the judge, shortly, as one who whistles to keep his courage up.

The doctor's fingers drummed on the table as he paused thoughtfully.

"Carshena," he said, "if you can believe me, measured out the kerosene oil he allowed for

each week on Monday ; and when it gave out
they went to bed at dusk, if it gave out on
Friday night. But one thing Adelia did manage to do. So long as a drop of oil was in the
measure a light stood in the window that lit
up that ugly turn in the county road round the
corner of their house. I know her light saved
me from a bad collision once ; some of you
also, perhaps. She's kept that little lamp so
clean it always shone like a jewel up there.
The window-pane it shone through had never
a speck on it either. That's what I call public spirit. And it's public spirit, too, that
made her keep sweet-smelling flowers growing on the top of the old road wall. In summer I always drive past there slowly to enjoy
them. When she comes on the charity of the
town she may console herself by remembering these things. She did what she could (in
spite of Carshena), and nobody can do more.
Here are the plans for his monument, gentlemen. I would like to have your vote on
them."

The little company, as if glad to move, drew
about the table while the doctor opened the
plans and laid them in a row. The butcher,
whose ruddy face looked dim in his disappoint-
ment, and whose despondent chin hung down

on his white shirt bosom, picked up one of the designs gingerly and examined it.

"Are they all alike, doctor?" he asked.

Judge Bowles looked over Mr. Gowan's shoulder.

"Each design seems to be a hollow shaft of some kind, with a round opening at the top," he said, and looked inquiringly over his glasses at the doctor, who nodded assent.

"They are all hollow. You seem to get more for your money so. The round opening at the top of the shaft can be filled with anything we may choose later. I might suggest a crystal with the virtues of the deceased inscribed on it. Then, if we keep a light burning behind the glass at night, those virtues will shine before us by night and by day."

Judge Bowles lifted his eyes quickly. The doctor's face was unpleasantly satiric, and his blue eyes looked out angrily from under his curling white hair. Judge Bowles sat down, leaning back heavily in his chair, his perplexed eyes still on Dr. Michel's frowning brow. Mr. Gowan, with a look as near anger as he could achieve, moved to a seat behind the stove. His idol was failing him utterly. He felt he himself could have done better than this. Dr. Michel's roving eyes glanced round the circle

" ' THEY ARE ALL HOLLOW ' "

top of the monument. I spoke of a crystal set in that opening, with the virtues of the deceased inscribed upon it, but we can, if we choose, carve those same virtues in the more imperishable stone below, and print something else—a clock face perhaps—on the crystal above. That's a mere minor detail."

Judge Bowles, whose gaze had been growing more and more bewildered, now started in his chair and sat suddenly upright. He stared at the doctor uncertainly. The doctor cast a quick look at him, and went on rapidly :

" If you will allow me, I'll make my report and leave it with you. I have a great deal to do this morning in other directions. It has occurred to me that as the base of the monu-ment is to be square and hollow, it would be easy to fit it into a comfortable living-room, with one, or perhaps two, small rooms built about it. I have not mentioned this to the architect, but I know it can be done. The will especially directs that repairs and care be allowed for." The doctor was talking very rapidly now. " The monument will not cost more than ten thousand, the clock about two. Twelve thousand from twenty thousand leaves eight thousand. The yearly interest on eight thousand and the fact that we could offer free residence in the monument should let us engage a reliable resident keeper, who would give the time and attention that such a monument and such a park would need."

The doctor paused, and again looked about him.

The whole circle of faces looked back at him curiously—some with a puzzled gaze, but several, including Judge Bowles, with a half-fascinated, half-dismayed air. Mr. Gowan alone preserved his look of utter hopelessness.

"Who'd take a job like that?" he said, gloomily. "I wouldn't, for one, live in a vault with Carshena, dead or alive."

"Oh, the grave could be outside, and the monument as a kind of monster head-stone," said the doctor, pleasantly. "My idea was to have the grave well outside. Four or five hundred and a home isn't much to offer a man, gentlemen, but I happen to know a very respectable elderly female who would, it seems to me, suit us exactly as well as a man. In fact, I think it would considerably add to the picturesque features of our little town park to have a resident female keeper. I think I see her now, sitting in the summer sunshine at the door of this unique head-stone monument, or in winter independently luxuriating in its warm and hospitable shelter. I see her winding the clock, affectionately keeping the grave like a gorgeous flower-bed, caring for the shrubbery, burnishing the clock lamp till it shines like a jewel, as she well knows how to do, and best of all in her case, gentlemen, I happen to know from her own lips that she has no fear of ghosts. Why, gentlemen, what's the matter? I protest, gentlemen."

At that moment Mr. Gowan might be said to be the doctor's only audience. The rest of the company were engaged in whispering to each other, or speechlessly giving themselves over to suppressed and unholy glee. Judge Bowles was openly wiping his eyes and shaking in his chair. Dr. Michel looked around the circle with resentful surprise.

"You seem amused, gentlemen!" he said, with dignity; and then addressing himself to Mr. Gowan exclusively, as if that gentleman alone were worthy to be his listener, "Would you object to a woman as keeper, Mr. Gowan?"

"What's her name?" asked the butcher.

A roar of laughter, not to be longer suppressed, drowned his words. Mr. Gowan looked about the shaken circle, stared for a moment, then suddenly, as comprehension, like a breaking dawn, spread over his round face, he brought his hand down hard on his fat knee.

"Well, doctor," he roared, in admiration too deep for laughter, "if you ain't the dawgorndest!"

The doctor's wiry hair seemed to rise and spread as wings, his eyes snapped and twinkled, his mouth puckered. "Will some one embody this in the form of a motion?" he asked, gravely. The judge dried his eyes, and, with difficulty, rose to his feet.

"Gentlemen," he said, "I move that we build this monument with a base large enough for a suite of rooms inside ; that we set this structure on the lot which our good doctor has chosen ; that we ornament it with an illuminated clock at the top ; and further, that—that this female keeper be appointed."

"Seconded, by Harry !" roared Mr. Gowan.

The doctor, with his hands on his hips, his body thrown far back, looked with the eye of a conqueror over the assembly. "Those in favor of the motion will please say Aye ; those opposed, No. It seems to be carried ; it is carried," he recited in one rapid breath.

"Amen !" endorsed Mr. Gowan, fervently.

And this warm approval of their butcher was in the end echoed as cordially by the most conservative citizens of Leonard. After the first shock of their surprise was over, natural misgivings were lost in enjoyment of the grim humor of this very practical jest of their good doctor's. Many a village has its park, and many a one its illuminated clock ; it was left for Leonard to have in its park a grave kept like a gorgeous flower-bed, and at the grave's head a towering monument that is at once a tombstone, an illuminated clock, and a residence for the park's keeper.

Who the next keeper may be it is one of the amusements of Leonard to imagine. The present incumbent is a happy old woman, whose fellow-citizens like nothing better than to see her, according to their doctor's prophecy, winding the clock, caring for the flowers, burnishing the town lamp ; in summer sitting in the sunshine at the door of the head-stone monument, in winter luxuriating in that warm and independent shelter.

" I feel as if Carshena knew just what was best for me, after all, doctor," she said to her physician, in his first call upon her in her new home ; and that worthy, with a nod of his white head, assented in the readiest manner.

" Doubtless, madam, doubtless," he said, " Carshena had all this in his mind when he made me his executor. Didn't you, Carshena?" He winked his eye genially at the grave as he passed out, and, with no shade of uncertainty or repentance in his mind, climbed into his buggy and went on his satisfied way.

OF HER OWN HOUSEHOLD

"BIANCA, do you see that little path?"

"Nonsense! There isn't any to see. I told you there wouldn't be."

"There is. Stand back here where I am and you'll see it."

A long pause.

"Two bodies can't possibly occupy the same place, Charles. Don't they teach natural science in France?"

"The most natural of all the sciences, dearest. Don't 'keep yourself so far removed,' as my uncle calls it."

"Then don't make it so necessary!"

"I won't move a finger—I swear I won't— if you'll come here and look at the path. You can't see it from where you stand in the dusk." Another pause, and a rustling of the weeds and dry grass growing outside the neglected old grape-arbor. Then a girlish laugh.

"Oh, oh! I do see it. It leads straight from your uncle's house, and it looks for all the world like a little rabbit-path in the weeds. Do you really think he meets her out-doors here somewhere? How can they! They are so old."

"Everybody can't be as young as you and I."

"Oh, you said you wouldn't!"

"Well, I didn't. I only wanted to. How old is your grandmother?"

"I don't know; thousands of years old. How old is your uncle?"

"About that same age." Another pause.

"Just think of it! So old, and still having rabbit-paths worn towards her!"

"As for rabbit-paths, I expect to be keeping my rabbit-gun loaded long after your head is white, Bianca."

"Don't. I want to be sensible. Do you know, this will make an awful fuss if my parents and my uncles and aunts find it out."

"Then don't tell them. But I don't see why they should care. I wouldn't, for my part."

"You wouldn't like them to marry!"

"Why not?"

"Why—why—it would be so very bad for grandmamma. It would agitate her so." This time it was the man who laughed.

"Maybe she'd like to be agitated. Why should we care. We have enough on our own hands just now."

159

"Oh, but I would care. It would be so absurd. The family would all hate it; and I suppose your family in France would look on it as a terrible mésalliance, wouldn't they?"

"He wouldn't care how they looked on it. He'll never go back there again. He never has since he went back for me and the title. Besides, wouldn't that be a high note, when he was only a tutor for your grandmother's children once upon a time? He taught your own mother 'ze musique and ze languages.'"

"But that was long, long ago, before he became the Count Malleville with lots of money. He's richer than my grandmother now. I think he's bought half her plantation from her; and as for your new house over there, it would cast ours all in the shade if your trees weren't kind enough to hide it."

Again rang out the pretty, gurgling laugh of a very young girl.

"Oh, do you remember how grandmamma used to mimic him, and tell us about the time when he was a resident tutor here and wouldn't keep our American Sundays? 'Oh, Madame Outerbrook, Madame Outerbrook, it is to be your Sunday all ze day to-day. Well, I will go and rupticate my stockings.' And then when grandmother told him he really mustn't darn his

160

stockings on Sunday, 'Oh, Madame Outerbrook, we all get to ze heavens our own way.
Le bon Dieu, He understands. On zat last day
he will say, "Presbyterian, you go zare; Epis-
copalian, you go zare; Catholique, you go
zare; Monsieur Malleville—you go where you
please."'"

The two laughing young voices joined together in the last words, as if uniting in a well-
known recitative. Then the man's voice went
on alone:

"You mark my words, she's going to 'rupticate' his stockings for him from now on. Your
grandmother never mimicked him to me, Bianca. Of course she didn't I'm his nephew.
Don't you remember how you girls used to hide
me behind her chair and then tease her to
mimic him? I remember everything we ever
did together, dear. You are so beautiful, Bianca, and I do love you so." Another pause.
"Come, let's walk down by the pond where no
one else goes, and look for—"

"Frogs' legs, you Frenchman?"

"No; for our ancestors, and each other,
dearest."

The rustling of feet in the dry grass grew
louder, then fainter and fainter. Before all sound
died away the girl's voice came back clearly:

"Do you know, I think you must be right, for I haven't heard grandmamma mimic him in ages — not since we were all children together. Isn't it too funny? And it's kind of pathetic too. There'll be an awful fuss!"

"So we are to be opposed, it appears, my dear count," said Madam Outerbrook, looking up into her aged lover's face and laughing softly, but, alas, not as the young Bianca had laughed. They were sitting together in the old grape-arbor hand in hand, as the two young lovers had stood outside a few minutes before. There had been only some grape leaves between the two couples. Count Malleville replied by lifting the fragile but still beautiful old hand to his lips.

"Let them oppose," he said, sturdily, in his exact accent, which the young people had faithfully rendered a few moments before. "Let them oppose," he repeated, again kissing Madam Outerbrook's hand.

"Take care, dear friend," she replied, with spirit, and smiling up at him, "you might agitate grandmamma! So Bianca and Charles are in earnest, after all. Your nephew and my favorite grandchild. That ought to be very nice."

"It will be very nice," echoed Monsieur Malleville. "We might have—how do you call it?—a dooble wedding."

"Nonsense!" said Madam Outerbrook. She laughed, and colored a little before she went on, with feeling, "Ah, the young think the old cease to feel, Monsieur Malleville."

"To feel, one must have lived seventy years," said Monsieur Malleville, quickly; and Madam Outerbrook laughed aloud.

"In the liberal translation we call that 'No fools like old fools.' Sometimes I wonder if we are two old fools."

"I hope it," returned Count Malleville, earnestly—"I hope it;" and Madam Outerbrook laughed again.

"At least we are old enough to know our own minds," she said. "It is my family who will make the greatest objection, I fancy. Perhaps you would like me to assure you again that I am not to be shaken."

"I have already that assurance here," answered Monsieur Malleville, his hand on his heart. "But, my dear lady, now that our children suspect—you heard them talk of ze rabbit-path," he laughed, good-naturedly—"would it not be more dignified that we announce our intentions?"

"Perhaps," said Madam Outerbrook, thought-fully. "Yes, you are always right, my dear friend. It is better to be frank with them. To-night they will all be dancing in the house. The moonlight is gone for this month, and there will be nothing to take them outside. Shall we tell them to-night, when they are all together? Very well; that is decided."

Every summer it was the family custom that all of those who owed their being to Madam Outerbrook—to the remotest babe—should re-turn to her spreading roof for the hot season, and naturally there was each year a larger tribe returning; but in this particular summer, it having been a fruitful epoch in the never-barren Outerbrook family, they had crowded in, branch and twig and budding leaf, until the great old mansion was a veritable tent of Abraham. Because the children were so many more, or else her strength was less, Madam Outerbrook had never before been so unduly nervous concerning the safety of these soft small creatures that, like little tadpoles restored to their proper element, rioted all the hot day long over her old plantation. It seemed to her, too, that the children had never been so am-bitiously troublesome, while their parents had never been so recklessly careless of their safety; and it was then she contracted a habit that, as it grew upon her, was to wear on her nerves and tire her beyond words. She never knew quite how it began, but she suddenly found herself constantly and anxiously numbering the children. Whenever they came to their meals she counted them; and again—and most important—at night she would creep up the stairs and number them in their innocent sleep. There were always thirty - seven of them; and she was always heartily ashamed of her foolish fears, but this did not prevent their recurrence the next day and the next.

On the day of this history, engrossed in her own affairs, Madam Outerbrook had not once counted her brood, and that night they lay up-stairs unnumbered, away from the strains of music that gave other employment to the slippered feet of their young mothers, dancing below.

For there was dancing in the house that night, as Madam Outerbrook had prophesied there would be. All of the family proper, and most of their young neighbors also, were gathered together, as asked or unasked they always flocked into the great Outerbrook ball - room when the moon failed. Generally Madam Outerbrook was first in the ball-room to formally welcome her guests, for she believed in a due degree of formality ; but on this occasion the dancing was well under way before she made her appearance ; and when she did enter the hall it was leaning on the arm of Count Malleville, with whom she had walked the whole circle of the room before she seemed to find a chair to her liking. Count Malleville, too, though always scrupulously attired and ever ceremonious in manner, showed, both in his dress and bearing, an air as of preparation for some occasion. Added to these straws in the wind, Madam Outerbrook wore a set of jewels which at once brought on this whispered conversation in a corner of the room :

"Oh, Charles, do look ; do ! Grandmamma's not leaning on your uncle's arm ; she's *supported* by it, and she's got on her maiden jewels—the beautiful ones she brought with her into the family. She's always worn the Outerbrook jewelry my grandfather gave her since her marriage. And look at your uncle's face ! I do believe they've something to tell us to-night !"

"If they do, just as surely as I stand here, we'll follow it by announcing ours. Let's steal a march on them and announce ours first, Bianca. Come, tell them now."

"It's too late," said Bianca, looking across the room. "Look! Do you suppose grandmamma can be going to stand up there and announce it out loud!"

But no, though Madam Outerbrook had risen, it was only to hurry abruptly from the room. The sight in the ball-room of all these barenecked, bare-armed, laughing, careless, chatting young mothers—her own daughters—had given her a sharp reminder of the duty for once neglected. Count the children she must, let wait what would. She hurried up the stairs to a great bedroom which she had fitted into a kind of dormitory for all the younger children. It was a part of one of the two great wings of the house that, after one fashion of Southern homes, curved out like hospitable arms on either side of the main building. The apartment was very large, and there was nothing in it but beds ; some of them cradles, some little trundle-beds, that held one small child snugly, and some great four-posters, easily embracing four or five children, their bodies lying across the mattresses, their little heads, light and dark, bolstered in a row at the long sides. The big airy room was the prettiest of sights on these hot summer nights, when the tossing brood flung off their light coverlids and lay

with plump and naked arms and legs out-
stretched in their childish dreams. The grandmother could not understand why the children's own mothers so rarely toiled up the
stairs to enjoy this vision. In her tender eyes
no moonlight night was ever half so lovely, no
ball-room half so enchanting.

A little breathless with her haste, and holding up her heavy skirts bunched together in
the front, Madam Outerbrook began a hurried
counting of the flock. In her young days she
had had the care of her mother's poultry-yard,
and often as she stood thus in the big dormitory, or moved from aisle to aisle among the
beds, she thought of those other restless broods
she had with difficulty numbered over in their
coops. The sleeping children did not move so
distractingly as the chickens had moved, but
if she were tired, as she too often was now, she
would on a first count make them out one or
two more than thirty-seven or one or two less.
She was never satisfied until by two counts
they proved an odd thirty-seven. It did not
surprise her now that, with so much else of
vital moment on her mind, the children counted
but thirty-six on her first tally. She only began again more painstakingly and with less
hurry, moving from bed to bed, and examin-

ing the knobs under the covers that might be
heads or pillows. At the last cot her heart,
that for years had been beating less and less
strongly, began to throb sharply. The count
again was one short of thirty-seven. A thin
night taper shone in a corner of the room, and
lifting it in hands that trembled a little, she
made her round again, pausing long at each
bed. There were Minnie's two boys and one
girl ; there was John's boy safe enough ; there
should be a girl of John's too. No ; she was
grown now; she was Bianca, down-stairs dancing. Josie's big twins in this bed; her boy—
he too was old enough to be dancing down-
stairs. There should be thirty-seven children
without Bianca and Josie's boy. Madam Outerbrook's head began to swim. All the while she
was confusedly trying to sort out her lost lamb,
if one were lost, she was seeing shocking visions
of some one of these well-worshipped little
bodies lying pitifully in the bottom of the pond,
or smothered in her barn, or lost perhaps in her
stable in some more horrible fashion. It seemed
to her at first impossible to identify her loss,
but she was of a generation of fighters, and en-
durance came in her blood, thin if it now was.
The little taper was still burning, forgotten in
her hand, when, white as a sheet, she walked

across the brilliantly lit ball-room; but her step was steady, and she knew which astonished daughter to stand before, and just which grandchild to demand of her.

"Katherine, when did you last see Jimmy Dick?"

"Oh, mercy, mother, what is the matter? I saw him—why, I saw him—I saw him—"

"Did you see him at supper?" asked Madam Outerbrook, sternly.

"I—I was out driving."

"Did you see the child at dinner?"

"I—I don't remember. His nurse must have seen him. Isn't he in bed?"

"He is not in bed," answered Madam Outerbrook, sharply. "Somebody bring me the child's nurse."

Somebody brought the child's nurse to the ball-room, while all the mothers streamed wildly in their gay attire up the stairway and into the curved wing, identifying their own offspring. The grandmother had made no mistake. It was Jimmy Dick who was missing, and no search in any convenient spot revealed him. It appeared there had been, for some reason, a "swapping" of charges among the nurses at dinner-time, and again at supper, and in the change Jimmy Dick had been "mislaid."

Such was the nurse's story. A little further inquiry left no possibility of doubt that Jimmy Dick, aged four, had been mislaid since his morning bath, and this fact once established, the wildest confusion reigned. Half-dressed, half-crying children, brought down in their parents' arms, were hurriedly questioned. The scared faces of the negro nurses grew the more ashy under cross-examination. It was all useless. No one knew anything whatever of Jimmy Dick. Madam Outerbrook, a commanding if trembling figure, stood in the centre of the polished floor, issuing her orders.

"Ring the bell!" ordered the mistress of the plantation. "Have out every negro in the quarters. Light torches and get lanterns. Nobody shall sleep or eat until the child is found."

In the house she set the women servants to work turning over every article of furniture, every bed and closet. Out-doors negro men's voices were calling the child's name, the soft gloom broken by their moving torches and lanterns. Madam Outerbrook could not head the search in body, but she did in brain and spirit.

"Get up, Katherine!" she said, sternly, to the child's mother sobbing at her feet. "This is no time to cry." And rising obediently, Kather-

171

ine choked down her sobs, following the grandmother from room to room, from veranda to
veranda, from garden walk to garden walk.

"Come and rest, my child," said Madam
Outerbrook, more gently at last. "We have
looked in every spot that you and I can reach.
Don't give way, Katherine; they may find him
outside. Here is Count Malleville. Ah, my
dear, faithful friend, how exhausted you look!
Do you bring any news? None? They have
beaten out all the corn - fields — the tangle?
Yes, and the wheat-fields?"

Count Malleville, toiling at the head of the
searchers, had come back to say they and he
were satisfied that the child was not on the
plantation. He looked at Madam Outerbrook
with an anxious look in his kind eyes.

"Madame, I hate to suggest it, but—they—
they—do you permit that—"

"Tell them to drag the pond," said Madam
Outerbrook, desperately, turning away as she
spoke. For the first time since the child's loss,
yielding to weakness, she stumbled and fell
forward heavily against the side of the house.
As she did so she drew back with a terrified
cry. A great roll of matting, taken up from
the floor of the ball-room and thrust out of the
way upon the veranda floor, had lain between

her and the wall, and at the touch of her foot the roll started and turned. With piercing cries it rolled over and over under their astonished gaze, while in their bewildered ears it still wailed louder and louder, angry, frightened cries, which doubled in volume as the great bundle turned on and over the edge of the veranda to drop on the soft grass below. There, turning still, it fell apart; while from what had been the hollow centre of the roll rose a hungry, cross, and sleepy little boy— Jimmy Dick—upon whom, tossing off the veranda exactly as the matting had rolled, fell Jimmy Dick's mother, laughing, crying, scolding, and calling out to the others even as she fell. In a moment she was surrounded by those who, like her, were at once laughing, crying, and scolding. Then the whole cavalcade disappeared almost as quickly as it had gathered, carrying off the central figures into the house.

Jimmy Dick had only been drowsy — who was not in this hot weather? — and seeing a hole, he had crawled into it, to sleep a trifle too well. That was all. The servants were recalled, the children dismissed to their beds; and in a time incredibly short, floating out to the veranda to Madame Outerbrook's sore ears, came the sound of reviving music.

"Where is grandmamma?" "Where can mother be?" she heard asked within over and over, but she did not move or speak until the charming face of her favorite grandchild, Bianca, was framed in the open window that looked out from the ball-room. Then, though Count Malleville's arm was supporting her trembling frame, Madam Outerbrook only leaned forward to look back pathetically and entreatingly into Bianca's eyes. With a wondering gaze in return, in which rose a pretty dawning sympathy, Bianca slowly and silently withdrew, drawing the curtains together behind her.

"Grandmamma's all right," Madam Outerbrook heard her clear voice saying. "But she says she's a good deal shaken, and she wants to be let alone."

The two old lovers stood silent.

"My dear friend, will you look in at the window and see if my Katherine is in the room?" said Madam Outerbrook tremulously at last. Her voice sounded in her own ears like that of an old woman for the first time. Count Malleville stepped forward and looked in cautiously between the curtains.

"Yes," he said; "she is zare. She passes now before ze window. Would you be pleased to see her yourself, my dear lady?"

"She is not dancing!" exclaimed Madam Outerbrook, and Count Malleville hesitated. He was quite prepared to say whatever he thought would most soothe Katherine's mother, irrespective of truth, but he was not sure what she wanted. Madam Outerbrook seemed to read his hesitation, and with uncertain step came to his side. Taking the arm he instantly offered, and leaning heavily on it, she looked in through the curtains. There, waltzing and laughing, a little wildly perhaps in their reaction, were Katherine and her husband, dancing together. Madam Outerbrook looked long and earnestly at the whirling pair, then dropped the curtain and turned sharply away. As she did so she was face to face with Count Malleville in the dim light.

"Suppose," she began with difficulty, both lips and voice quivering—"suppose, dear friend, that we were to let our young people, Charles and Bianca, marry and — and live here in the centre of this—this house, and then—my dear, dear friend — couldn't you live in one of the curved wings and I in the other? Do—do you follow me?"

Monsieur Malleville drew nearer, and looked down quickly and silently into her agitated face. She spoke more steadily :

"I mean, would you be willing to—to close your house and live, not—not in mine, but in what would be the home of Charles and Bianca?"

Monsieur Malleville was still silent, and she went on distressedly: "It isn't that we can't feel as much as these young people. It isn't that at all. It's that we feel so much, oh, so much more than they! If only we had their strength of body and our power to feel! But we haven't, dear friend; no, we haven't. At least I find I haven't. Grandmammas shouldn't be agitated." She laughed, with a catch in her breath. "You in one wing, I in the other, our dear children dividing, uniting us— Don't— don't you follow me?"

Count Malleville's pause was but for a moment. The next, whatever his emotion, he had straightened himself and stood as erect as ever in his youngest days. His bearing was as proud as that of any ancestor of his house, his voice as tender and as enriched with feeling as if he were indeed his nephew Charles and she her granddaughter Bianca. "I follow you to ze grave, dear friend," he said, firmly and gently, "in whatever compacity ze wisdom of my dear lady shall have chosen."

APPLES OF GOLD

"A word fitly spoken is like apples of gold in pictures of silver."—PROV. xxv. ii.

"DISREPUTABLE weather!—simply disreputable!" murmured Mr. Atwood.

He looked out from under the comfortable shelter of his umbrella as he spoke.

The rain was falling from the heavens in whirling sheets of silver. From a roof just ahead of him the spouting had given up carrying off the flow. The water ran over it in streams, which the wind caught again and flung aside in the air, breaking them into raindrops once more.

Mr. Atwood paused and watched the tangle for a moment; then shrugging the collar of his heavy overcoat still higher, and dexterously grasping his umbrella handle close by the ribs, he struggled on.

Around the street corner, and approaching the point of the angle which Mr. Atwood was nearing, another figure was battling against the weather; but where the man showed a certain vigor and enjoyment in resistance, the woman—for it was a woman, and a young one—walked with a nervous rapidity, and an apparent heedlessness of the wind's efforts to turn her light umbreila inside out.

At the street corner the big steadily advancing umbrella and the little wavering one met with a crash which brought the respective owners to an abrupt stand. They disengaged their weapons, and peered out at each other through the mist.

"Celeste! Why, my dear child!" exclaimed Mr. Atwood.

He raised his hand quickly to his hat, but only to hold it in place, not in salute.

Civilities die a natural death in a whirlwind.

The gust of air seized the girl's bobbing umbrella, and settled the question of turning it wrong side out once and forever. In the same moment Mr. Atwood's covering swept over her like a great sheltering wing.

"Come here, child," he said; "there is room for one more in the ark. Throw that wreck of silk and whalebone in the gutter, and come under gingham for once in your life."

Celeste obeyed, taking his offered arm. Con-

versation was impossible until the corner was
passed where the four winds of heaven seemed
to have appointed a rendezvous. Then Mr.
Atwood looked down at his companion's costume and smiled.

"Thin shoes, new gloves, and a silk sieve
water-proof! May I ask, madame, where you
are going?"

"I am taking a walk," said the girl, speaking
for the first time.

Mr. Atwood laughed. "*Were* Celeste," he
corrected, "were. You are being taken home
now, my dear; there, I trust, to be well scolded,
as these many moons have lapsed since the
honey-moon."

He looked down suddenly at the hand on his
arm, then into the face by his side, where there
were drops of water which he did not think
were rain. The lips were as tremulous as the
hand.

"Old! Heavens, how old you make me
feel!" said Mr. Atwood, anxiously examining
the ribs of his umbrella. "Here you are, a
sedate matron, and I remember the first day I
visited your family, and caught you, a little tot,
with long shaving curls pinned to your yellow
pigtails to eke them out. You don't remember
it, but I do. You were a pretty child, Celeste.

You might have been a good one, too, if we had spoiled you less."

A great drop, which again was not rain, fell on Mr. Atwood's sleeve. Without turning he talked on. "What business have you to be out a day like this? The wind is enough to make you hoarse for a week, let alone the dampness. Here, take my handkerchief and tie it about your throat."

Celeste took the handkerchief he offered, with a little hysterical laugh.

"That is just like you," she said, openly drying her eyes. "Ignore, ignore, always ignore—appearances, always appearances!"

"I don't think you can quite quarrel with me on that score. Here I am walking up a thoroughfare with a weeping young woman clinging to my arm, and all the 'Quaker ladies' in the puddles staring at us. Could Mrs. Grundy ask for more?"

"Don't laugh," cried Celeste, hysterically, "pray don't!"

Mr. Atwood turned and stood quite still for a moment, looking into her face.

Then he lifted the umbrella slightly, and looked out from under it. They had been walking in the teeth of the storm, but now he altered their course to a cross street, where the inner edge of the farther pavement was comparatively sheltered.

"Now," he said, "we have miles of way before us. My handkerchief is a large one, and my reputation can stand it. You may tell me what it is if you wish, and if I can help you ; if not, you may cry your cry out with the weather, and then I will take you home."

They walked on in silence. At last Celeste spoke.

"I think," she said, thoughtfully—"I think that I shall tell you. I am so sorely in need of help, and the wind has blown you to me. My trouble is about my husband."

Mr. Atwood laid his hand quickly on the one in his arm. He shook his head, half smiling.

"No," he said, "the wind never meant that. It blew you to me because it knew I could be heartless enough to send you away without letting you speak. No, whatever it be, whether great or small, if it concerns your married life, tell no one. Fight it down. Put it behind you. Do anything but talk."

"Then you too fail me," said Celeste, bitterly.

Mr. Atwood's voice grew graver, his manner more serious.

"You must not misunderstand me. You know me as always devoted to your interests. I have no wish to learn your secret. My advice to you is to keep it. At the same time, if you need help, if you need me, I am here."

"I must have help," she answered, in a choked voice; "I have just discovered that my husband is a liar."

Mr. Atwood uttered an exclamation of incredulity. "A liar! Impossible, Celeste!"

"You thought it a lovers' quarrel, did you not? Now, will you listen? As you are a lawyer and a man of the world, you may understand."

"I am your old friend, and your husband's," he answered, gravely. "Some one has misled you maliciously."

"What I know I discovered myself."

"Then you are mistaken."

"No, I tell you I know it. He has been deceiving me for months. Do you suppose I accepted light evidence?"

Mr. Atwood was silent for a moment; then he spoke simply.

"You mean," he said, "that he has been unfaithful to you?"

Celeste lifted her head proudly, her color rising.

"No, that humiliation I am spared. My husband is still my husband."

The expression of troubled gravity on Mr. Atwood's face lightened.

"Then," he replied, with decision, "his wife must be his wife."

"I have made up my mind. I shall return to my mother," said Celeste, quickly.

Apparently Mr. Atwood did not hear her.

"What is it that has happened?" he asked.

Celeste flushed painfully. Her eyes dropped.

"How can I bring myself to tell it?" she cried, bitterly. "I am so ashamed! If it were not so contemptible!—its hideousness lies in its smallness."

There was almost a smile in Mr. Atwood's eyes as he looked down at her.

"Child," he said, half sadly, half whimsically, "men are not great."

She glanced up quickly.

"Ah, you have not heard yet. I have not told you. You know how my fortune is left to me?"

"Yes; by your father's will it was left you outright, was it not?"

"*Leaving* me outright you would better say," corrected the girl, with a laugh which was not good to hear. "I wish I had never seen a penny

183

of it. I have been reinvesting. My father's investments were too old-fashioned. You have no idea how easy it was; I had only to sign papers, and my husband did all the rest. I was to be troubled with nothing. Yesterday — it is the old story — my husband gave me a box of papers to assort, and among them I stumbled on a letter which I read twice before I understood. It was an acknowledgment of almost the exact amount I had last reinvested, dated the same day — one of my husband's debts of honor. His honor! I understood then why I was not to be troubled."

Whatever were Mr. Atwood's thoughts, they were not expressed in his face. His eyes were fastened on the lower points of his umbrella, from which the water dropped ceaselessly. His countenance was inscrutable.

"Had you no further evidence?" he asked, quietly.

"In plenty. It rolled up like a snowball. I have an unfortunate memory for dates and sums. Each one of my reinvestments antedated some settlements. Do you suppose I was easier to convince than you? Comparatively speaking, they all agreed."

"With what?"

"The other papers."

"The other papers? Ah, Eve—Eve. It has been so since the first little red apples were made. Child, I could almost wish you had remained ignorant: the tree of knowledge bears such bitter fruit. Yet, sooner or later it must have come."

"I have been thinking that it would be best for me to go first to my mother's house, and from there make my plans," said Celeste, with the same high-strung composure.

"Once," answered Mr. Atwood, thoughtfully, "I knew a woman — a devoted wife — whose husband was the most scientific brute with whom I ever came in contact. After years of torture I induced her to sue for divorce for her children's protection. His party — he inevitably has one, you know—maintained that the root of all the trouble lay in the fact that she never had cared for him, and they found listeners."

"I shall go to my mother," repeated Celeste, firmly.

"And your children?"

"I shall take them with me."

"And if your husband claim them?"

"I should contest it."

"In court?"

"In court, if necessary."

185

"And are you sure that in after years they will thank you—even if by so doing you rescue their property?"

"That would not be my motive," she interrupted.

Mr. Atwood went on, unheeding. "They might, perhaps, prefer their mother's and father's unspotted name to riches. Children have an odd habit of resenting these things in after life. I have heard parents complained of as handicaps often enough to wish that children could select them for themselves."

Celeste's lip curled.

"How civilized we are!" she said, scornfully. "You repeat your little bon - mots ; I smile ; we walk on with my life's problem under discussion, and it strikes neither of us as odd."

"Yes, we are very civilized ; but would you have us otherwise ? Would it be really better if I told you with brutal directness that the world draws small distinction between a woman who returns of choice to her family and a woman *returned?* Suppose I pointed out to you baldly that there are always two sides told to a story ; that tongues in plenty would say you should have given the money ; and, finally, that your children may live to curse the day when their mother published their father's shame—would that be better?"

He could feel that she winced.

"Exposure would not be necessary. He could trust to my silence. I am in a position to dictate terms, I think. Let him take the bulk of the property. All I ask of him is that I may be allowed to go quietly, and take my children with me."

"And what has he answered?"

"Nothing as yet. When I met you I had come out from the house to breathe and think how best to speak to him."

Mr. Atwood turned so sharply that he almost faced his companion.

"Do you mean that you have not yet spoken to your husband?"

"Not yet; I shall to-night."

"Thank Heaven!" said Mr. Atwood, fervently. "Thank Heaven, my dear child! Celeste, your good angel watched over you."

She laughed, mirthlessly.

"Over me!—me! If I have such an one, 'peradventure he sleepeth, or he is on a journey.' If an innocent woman was ever delivered into the hands of the unrighteous, I have been."

"No, you are saved, you and your children.

Your husband must never know of your discovery."

Celeste looked up in amazement. " Leave him and give no reason ! It would not be possible."

" No, that would not be possible ; but this will. You must go back to your home and your husband, resolved to pick up your life in silence where you meant to lay it down. It is your only chance for happiness, and for your children's future."

As she grasped his meaning, Celeste withdrew from him with a gesture almost of abhorrence.

" Do you realize what this is that you are telling me to do?" she asked. " I who have never known what a lie was ! You are telling me to live one from now until I die—to make my whole life a masque—to act a part day by day and hour by hour."

Her eyes filled with passionate tears. Her voice broke.

" It is your hard part to play," said Mr. Atwood, slowly, " but you will play it."

" Never !"

" You will play it for your children and for your children's father. Where others love to remember, you must learn to forget. Where others unfold their heart's secrets, you must wrap yours away. It will be cruelly hard at first. It will tax all your strength, all your high spirit ; but you will succeed."

"Let me understand," said Celeste, in a repressed voice, " just what you are mapping out for me."

"I want you to wipe yesterday and to-day out of your life, letting no one suspect—hardly admitting to yourself—that they have made a difference. Train yourself to forget, forgiveness will follow."

Celeste shook her head.

"No, I could never forget. I can forgive, but it must be from a distance. I cannot live with him. I cannot be his wife and the mother of his children."

"Yet you are both, irreparably. You have put your hand to the plough, and you may not look back. You have come out from your people ; you have formed a household of your own. You have no moral right now to let it drop apart."

"And you think it could be bound together with a lie ?"

Mr. Atwood smiled.

"There spoke your Puritan grandparents. The Truth—the Te-ruth, in two syllables—a

189

trifle through the nose—and at any cost. Why
not the Truth of Saint Francis : ' Better to
withhold than to speak unkindly?' Let me ask
you one question. You have assured me that
your husband cares for no other woman—but
does he still care for you ?"

"Can you call this caring ?"

"Perhaps. I know that yours was a love-
match to begin with. Would you have said
yesterday, before this discovery, that there
had been any change in your husband?"

" No-o," she answered, hesitatingly ; "there
had been no change on the surface."

"And you ?"

He felt her arm tremble in his. There was
no answer, and he repeated his question. Her
voice faltered perceptibly.

" Can you wonder that my respect is dead?"

" And your affection ?"

"I told you that my respect was dead. My
love could never live without respect to feed
it."

"And yet I have known fatally numerous
affections that throve on less, and without the
excuse of marriage. I am not asking if you
forgive or if you respect. I ask if you still care
for your husband as he is ?"

The rain dropping monotonously on the um-

190

brella was the only break in the silence. Celeste spoke wearily at last.

"Yes, I still care. But it only makes it all harder—more impossible—more miserable."

She broke down suddenly, weeping softly.

"Oh, I have loved him—and, indeed, he loved me. I would have given him everything. How could he—ah! How could he wreck it all!"

Mr. Atwood let her weep on in silence, until her self-control again asserted itself. Then he spoke.

"There shall be no wreck, dear child. Take courage; you will come to the rescue. If I could promise you your first ideal of love and life I would. As it is, I can only help you to a second best, and with narrower limits perhaps. But then the worm has to be content in its chestnut, and what are we but worms?"

"How good you are, and how you understand!" she whispered. "I will try—indeed, I will try. Whatever you tell me I will do," she added, humbly.

Mr. Atwood's eyelids dropped for a moment. He bent over Celeste's bowed head, and opened his lips to speak; then, with a sudden change, laid his hand on hers, drawing it farther through his arm. He turned in the direction opposite to the one which they were taking.

"Then our first steps in the right path will be towards home," he said, cheerfully. "We can reach it quickly from here by cross-streets, and my first orders are very practical. You áre to put on dry slippers and a warm gown, and to send for a cup of hot tea."

She smiled sadly. "If that were all! And then?"

"Then the next is practical also, if not so easy. This leakage of your property must be stopped at once."

Celeste made an impatient gesture. "That is the last point to consider."

"No, it is the first. Remember, I have known your husband as long as you have, perhaps longer; and I know him as one man knows another. He will not enter into obligations with no means of meeting them; he did not before marrying you. When he comes to you again you must speak as lovingly and gently as you can, but with decision. Tell him you feel it is wronging his children to transfer such large sums on the judgment of one mind; that you would be more content if some one else were consulted—any one he chooses to name, provided he have knowledge on such subjects. The objection would be too reasonable, the condition too generous, to be cavilled at. He will consent, and, if I know him at all, suggest that you name a friend of your own. In that case, the person most natural for you to mention would be myself. He will not be likely to lay a reinvestment before me of which I would not approve."

There was no sarcasm in his voice, and she looked up with quick humiliation to read it in his face, but in vain. With a sudden realization that this was the initiation of her part, she uttered a broken exclamation, as of physical pain.

"No, no, it is impossible ; you overrate my strength."

As Mr. Atwood looked down at what had been a face formed for all that was hopeful and loving, and saw it now, twisted with emotion, his eyebrows contracted, and a deep cleft grew between them. He spoke with extreme gentleness :

"Celeste, if there were any other way in the world I should never insist on one which is so repugnant to you, but there is no other. If you destroy your husband's belief in your belief in him, you rob him of anything to live up to in life. When you withdraw the copestone of his self-respect, you set that of his ruin. He could never look you in the face again. You

N   193

would lose everything and gain nothing. Your strength is to sit still.   And besides—"

He paused and hesitated, then smiled the kindly, half-whimsical smile peculiar to him.

"I may as well say it.   Suppose, to-day, every loving wife in the world confessed to her husband the exact estimate at which she rated his characteristics in the tribunal of her secret soul, how many homes would be left standing to-morrow do you think?   We demand that our women admire us.   It is an innocent vanity, but I wonder if you know how deep are its roots?"

Again Celeste smiled sadly.

"You have conquered once more," she said, sighing, "and none too soon.   There are my door-steps.   Yes, I will try, and if I fail, or if I succeed, I shall always be grateful to you."

"You will not fail.   Nature did not give you that prominent little chin for nothing, my child."

"No," she answered, thoughtfully, "I think that I shall not fail."

They walked up the wet marble steps in silence.   Mr. Atwood rang the bell, and they stood in the sheltered vestibule, with that strangeness already creeping in which must come sooner or later after hearts have been laid open.

"There is one thing more," said Mr. Atwood; "all that has been said by you to me and by me to you under this circle of gingham must be closed with its closing—and forever. I shall never refer to it again, nor must you."

"I understand," she answered, simply.

The servant's footsteps sounded within, coming down the hallway towards the door. Celeste held out her hand, and as he took it in his, with a gesture which had no touch of gallantry in it, Mr. Atwood raised it to his lips.

"You will succeed," he repeated. The door opened — the harness of conventionality was adjusted.

"You will come in?" said Celeste, with an interrogation which meant nothing.

"No," he responded, in the same manner, "not now. Remember, Celeste, dry shoes and a warm gown and a cup of hot tea."

"I shall forget nothing."

He hurried her gently through the open door.

"And you are not to stand in the draught, either," he added, smiling. "Farewell!"

"Farewell," she replied. Her lips opened as

if she would have spoken further, but the door closed.

Mr. Atwood stood for a moment on the door-steps outside. His lower lip was caught between his teeth, and the upper one curled slightly. The same deep cleft appeared between his brows.

"No, I shall never forgive him," he muttered, as he descended the steps, "never — but you will. It was not about a woman that he lied to you."

MATILDA'S ADDRESS-BOOK

" Done it this time," said Joseph, coolly.

"Well, I should say you had," retorted his brother, rushing to the side of the boat and looking down. " Hard aground. Next time I let you sail my boat you'll know it."

" 'Tain't yours ; only half of it."

" Well, you sha'n't sail my half. Run aground in deep water on a rock you knew was here ! I tell you, you did know."

" Any harm done, boys ?" asked Marcus Garrett, with a calmness which was commendable in view of the fact that a glance showed him that the shore was well beyond his limited swimming powers.

" Naw," replied Joseph, with the same phlegm he had shown when the sail-boat first struck the rock gratingly, quivered, and then stood still. " Naw, Robert's just talking to hear himself. This old boat's banged on every rock in the lake. There ain't any easier rock to get off than this one."

197

"That's so," said Robert, with restored good-humor. "It's so big we can get off and walk on it and shove the boat off. It's the funniest old rock, anyhow—just like a table. The water ain't up to your knees anywhere."

"Deep enough at the edges," warned the older brother. "You want to be careful not to walk off it if you don't like a ducking. This is about the deepest part of the lake, I guess. We'll all have to pull off our shoes and stockings; then we can shove her off in no time. You'd better push your stockings into your pockets, Mr. Garrett, and tie your shoe-strings together and hang your shoes over your neck, like mine. You never know what'll happen. That's it. Now!"

A few moments later they were all three out on the table-like rock, up to their ankles in water, with shoes off and trousers rolled up, pulling and pushing and tugging at the heavy boat.

"There she goes, she's off!" shouted Robert, as the boat lurched suddenly and righted herself.

"Look out! Don't fall off the rock!" cried Joseph, in the same breath, and, heeding the warning, Marcus Garrett drew back hastily to safety. The next moment he was fairly rubbing his amazed eyes. How the lads had done it he was a trifle too far past his own boyhood to exactly know, but somehow, at a word from one of them, there was a rush and a bound, a flashing of bare white legs over the gunwale, a thumping of bare feet on the wooden decks, a squealing of ropes and a tightening of the sail, and the boys and the boat were well away from the rock with its solitary occupant. It never occurred to Marcus but that they would immediately return for him. Even when he saw the sail-boat heading for the farther shore, and observed the relentlessly immovable backs of two tousled heads against the sail, he still believed this to be one of those mysterious manœuvres of sail-boats whereby they attain their destination though heading in every direction save the place they are bound for. But as he stood there on the rock patiently waiting for the boys' return, a sudden flush spread up and over his face that he felt extended down to his very feet, plunged as they were in the cool bosom of the lake. The deliberation and the enormity of this outrage was in that moment apparent to him, for a familiar air came floating back to him from the disappearing boat. The air, not the words, was perfectly clear to Marcus. Familiar as the refrain was,

he could not at the moment place it; but that
it was sung derisively, and sung to mock him,
was only too plain.

Though a degree of innocence had betrayed
him into this position, Marcus was not so innocent as to believe there was still a chance
of his merciless tormentors relenting or returning for him. Why they had thus chosen
to pillory him he could not decide. He could
only wait for a chance rescue, praying that
it might come shortly, and not in a shape to
render his position more intolerable than it already was. While he was still hot and angry,
it was easier to stand, stork-like, first on one
foot and then on the other, upon a rock submerged in half a foot of water; but as time
went on, and his wrath grew less vehement,
Marcus distinctly felt the loss of its support.
Nobody was looking at him, but, then, at any
time anybody, *somebody*, might come drifting
around the nearest promontory and discover
him standing, like St. Peter, on the surface of
the waters, the only visible protuberance on
that wide expanse, his means of support quite
invisible to any casual eye.

As there was not enough wind to seriously
ruffle the waters, and as the lake was too fre-
quented for him to be left long on his watery

perch, Marcus was aware that he lacked even that dignity which belongs to danger, and it occurred to him that he would do well to employ his time in deciding which way he might look least ridiculous when rescued—whether he preferred to be discovered erect and motionless or wading about on his prison confines. He had just decided that the former attitude might be taken as an effort at dignity, which would, his judgment told him, be fatal, and he was stooping to cautiously feel his way about in the water when the splashing of a quick paddle near by struck his ear, and he looked up. As he looked he knew that the worst that could have befallen him had indeed befallen him.

In a canoe not far from him sat Matilda, wide-eyed and erect with amazement, her paddle poised in her hands, breathless in her astonishment. Marcus stood erect also and faced her, while for the moment neither of them spoke, and during this brief pause in our narrative it becomes imperative to leave our hero literally cooling his heels, and devoutly wishing the waters might rise and swallow him, while we explain why it was that this which had befallen him was indeed the worst.

The secret of this whole affair, which had

begun early in the summer, lay in the fact that Marcus had discovered that Matilda was not so old as she thought she was. Most women grow older as time passes, but there are a few exceptions to this rule. Matilda, unknown to others and to herself, had been for some time before this discovery steadily growing younger. The two facts that she was the youngest and the plainest of a large family of handsome daughters had held Matilda back in the nursery and the school-room. Thus she had formed the habit of maturing slowly, and, after some years experience in the social world, was apparently a grown woman, while in reality still nothing but an awkward school-girl. She was twenty-six years old, and her own belief that she was a confirmed celibate had taken an active form— of which we shall speak later—when it fell to the lot of Marcus Garrett to discern that Matilda, whom every one else thought a woman, and who surely was a woman in years, was only then on the verge of budding girlhood.

The manner of his awakening to this exciting discovery was in a way remarkable, though bearing the usual family likeness to all other such adventures. On that fateful day he was lazily floating about in a canoe, paddling to and fro with no thought of direction, when he

looked up to find that he had wandered from
the accustomed but unbeaten boat-paths to
that side of the lake where few cottages were,
and where here and there in the quiet lagoons
were dotted little fishermen's lodges, built by
the first summer settlers and now more or less
deserted. On the lonely porch of one of these
lodges—it was hard to say if it were a porch or
a wharf—sat a solitary female figure, whom
Marcus did not at once recognize, and when he
did see that it was Matilda he had stumbled
upon, he was distinctly regretful—the more so
that it was plain she had also recognized him,
and it was scarcely possible for him to withdraw as speedily as he desired without some
exchange of civilities.

" Good-morning," said Matilda, in answer to
his salutation, and—on such frail threads do our
fates hang—it was made plain to Marcus in
those two simple words that his companionship
was not desired. There is in the repertoire of
all women, however simple, this salutation final
and the salutation which invites. Matilda's
was so plainly the former that a mild curiosity
seized Marcus Garrett as to what on earth a
personage so unimportant as Matilda always appeared could be doing that made her wish to
be alone. As he drew nearer he distinctly saw

her draw a fold of her drapery over something that was hidden in her lap, and with this incentive, and with little else to amuse him that morning, Marcus steered his canoe to the side of the wharf-porch, stepping out lightly into that fate which awaited him.

Matilda was dressed in a white, soft gown, with little pink roses climbing all over it, and there were pink ribbons on her wide hat and at her waist. Her cheeks were pink also, and her skin a pretty sunburned brown, except behind her small ears, where it was very white, with little curls of light hair veiling it. Altogether she was a very pretty picture, and though he had met her many times before, for the first time Marcus glanced twice at her. She looked to him different, somehow. He decided that she was perhaps better dressed than usual, and then, as she did not ask him to sit down, which he would probably have refused to do if asked, he dropped at her side on the wharf, dangling his feet over the water as she was doing.

"What are you about here, all alone?" he asked.

"Not any harm," replied Matilda, smiling.

"I'm not so sure you are doing no harm," said Marcus. "What's that you are hiding in your lap?"

"My lap!" Matilda looked down, innocently. "Oh, this; it's nothing but my Address-Book."

She held up a fat little volume, as she spoke, that had a small brass label with "Address-Book" engraved on it. A small brass clasp held the covers together. Marcus stretched out his hand to take the book, which Matilda did not hold against·him, but which she evidently only refrained from doing through shyness or politeness. Marcus knew that he himself was not acting with perfected civility, but he was rather curious to see this hidden book, and no one ever considered Matilda's rights particularly.

"I don't believe this is an Address-Book," said Marcus, suspiciously turning the volume over. "I believe you are an authoress, and you are stealing off here to compose. This book is a manuscript. Now, isn't it?"

"It's nothing of the kind," retorted Matilda, indignantly. "I pledge you my honor it's an Address-Book and nothing else."

"Then if it's an Address-Book only, I can read it."

"I'm not so sure," said Matilda, coolly, and after an attempt to open the book Marcus was not so sure either, for the little brass clasp re-

sisted his fingers. On looking closely he could
see a small key-hole in its side. He glanced up
to find, to his further surprise, that Matilda
was laughing at him.

"Here's the key," she said. "It's on my watch-
chain, but you can't have it. I can't imagine
why you should care to see dry old addresses,
but if you really want me to read you a page or
two, give me the book and I'll do so. No, you
can't read it to yourself. If the sun wasn't so
nice and hot to-day, and the air so sweet and
cool, and that water so pretty and blue, and
those trees so green and brown, I don't believe
I would open the book at all. As it is, I feel
as if I could read you a little of it."

Marcus tried not to show her how she surprised him. Every one he had ever known,
however silent in other directions, had, as it
were, their pet subject on which they would
discourse if they could be gently led towards
it, and Marcus was rather clever in that kind
of leading. In this case he felt that he had
somehow dropped accidentally into Matilda's
pet subject, though he could not quite make
out what this subject was. Certainly she was
not now as she usually was, and the change was
to her—and he began to believe might prove
to his—advantage.

"Now this doesn't interest you, does it?" asked Matilda.

She had taken back her book, and, unlocking the clasp, turned over the pages a little, then read aloud :

"'Mr. —— addressing Miss ——: Dearest, I—I—I—I—' Why, how perfectly ridiculous! That was I, stammering. It's not so in the Address-Book," said Matilda, closing the volume, her cheeks very pink indeed. "You can finish this page for yourself, if you like. Only don't read any more."

But Marcus, though he took the open book she handed him, received it in a mechanical hand, and remained stupidly staring at her until Matilda blushed again even more deeply than she had as she read, or tried to read, the manuscript address.

"I suppose you are thinking I am a fool," she said, humbly, "and I don't know but I am, only I know I have had that book for years, and I never before was fool enough to try to read it to any one. Indeed, I had that plate made, with 'Address-Book' engraved on it, so no one would guess what the book really was. I thought of calling it my 'Hymn-Book,' but decided on this name finally. I think the hot sun must have affected my head to-day. What made you come in here this morning? Nobody ever comes in here."

Something was affecting Marcus, he knew, though he could not so exactly define what it was. Perhaps it was the sun. He only knew that blushing became Matilda to extravagance. She looked sixteen, and she talked with a delightful freshness and immaturity. Then, too, this curious and significant collection—what did it mean?

"May I ask," said Marcus, timidly, "if you have collected and written down here all the addresses which you yourself have received?"

"Dear me, no!" said Matilda, hastily. "Nobody ever offered themselves to me. These are other people's offers, and you don't know how hard they have been to collect. Almost every one vows they can't remember what they said, or what was said to them. I don't know whether that's true or not, because of course I haven't any way of gainsaying them, and then, too, I never have asked anybody leading questions. If any one happened to tell me how they got engaged, or if I heard it in any other way, I collected it."

She looked at Marcus with that appeal in her eyes which bespeaks the true collector's spirit, and which is more insistent than any leading question ever can be.

"Well," said Marcus, hurriedly turning from that phase of the subject, "people have collected everything else on earth, so why not addresses? Only I can't imagine what suggested them to you as collectable; and why didn't you finish the one you began to read to me?"

Matilda paused a moment before she replied.

"I think I could read you a funny one," she answered. "But that one I began was a serious one—one of my best. I don't know why I couldn't finish it."

"I know," said Marcus, boldly. He was recovering his wonted self-respect. "And you will after you grow up. Why, you are nothing but a child, a perfect child still. How old are you, anyhow?"

"Twenty-six," said Matilda, meekly.

"Twenty - six, and I'm twenty - eight," said Marcus; which latter fact seemed to have nothing whatever to do with the former until the words were uttered. Then Marcus, who was not a tyro, felt that he flushed slightly, and knew that something had happened, or was about to happen, which might prove of importance to him. It was merely a question of how deep or how shallow was the impression he was receiving, and this is not always an easy question for any man to settle at first blush. On looking back at this conversation, he always felt that Matilda's next few words were what brought him to that point where he knew his own mind only too well.

"You are very easy to talk to," said Matilda, with what he could not have thought simplicity in another woman, "and I am so glad you are, for I was just sitting here wishing I had some one to talk to and advise me a little. I've done something dreadful, and I'm going to tell you about it. Did you notice anything queer about my face to-day?"

"Queer?" repeated Marcus, gazing at her wonderingly. "No."

"Well, look hard at me and you will."

Now to be called upon to look hard into a soft and earnest upturned face is not the safest of offered contracts, as Marcus knew from practical experiences, but he promptly did as requested, and it was from that moment that he himself dated his captivity.

"I don't see anything *queer*—" he began, but Matilda interrupted him.

"It's perfectly wonderful. I can hardly believe it myself, it's so natural, but, do you know, I'm painted like a Jezebel, and I feel like one!

I knew you'd be horrified, but indeed I didn't mean to do it. You'll never tell if I tell you? We had a lot of company—girls—staying with us for the hotel hop last night, and I happened to run back into one of the rooms—I'll never tell which one—for something after they were all down-stairs, and there on one of the dressing-tables was a little tiny platter of red paint. She had forgotten to put it away, you see, and I can't imagine why I ever did such a thing, but I just wanted to see how it would look, and I daubed a little bit of it on one cheek, and then I couldn't get it off to save my life. I washed and I washed, and I scrubbed and scrubbed, and if you look you'll see it's on yet. Now comes the worst of it. I was so scared, and they were calling and calling me to come down-stairs, and I was so afraid they'd come up and catch me, and I couldn't go down as I was, so I just daubed the other cheek too, and then I went down-stairs. But the very worst of it all is, I—I—I got lots of attention at the hop last night. I—I liked it too, and I know it was only because of that dreadful paint, for I never had attention before. I am dreadfully afraid I may do it again some time. I don't think I shall, but I feel I might. And then here's my Address-Book. I couldn't go on keeping a collection like this if people were to be really attentive to me. It wouldn't be nice or delicate at all, would it? Do you think it immoral to paint?"

It is ever thus. Discoveries are rarely made singly. A moment before Marcus had been pluming himself on the fact that he was the first explorer, and now it seemed he might have rivals. The pretty pink color which he had noted and admired as he joined her was peculiarly becoming to Matilda, and was undoubtedly the source of her last night's triumphs. But as the bee forgets the perfume and the color which has invited him after he once tastes the honey, so it was with Marcus.

"Immoral!" he said, gravely. "Of course it's immoral to paint. I don't like to tell you how immoral painting is. I would speak more plainly if I were not sure you would never do so again. But I am sure."

"I never will," said Matilda, in an awed voice.

"And," Marcus went on, cruelly, "a little vaseline will at once take off any paint that's still on your face from last night. Water does no good."

"Oh," said Matilda, weakly, "thank you. I

will use the vaseline just as soon as I go home."

"But there's no hurry about going home yet, is there?" said Marcus.

"No," she answered, "and it's very nice here, isn't it? I come here in my canoe nearly every morning. This is our old fishing-lodge, and I keep the key of it. I sew and read and write in the house back there."

Marcus looked at her closely, but could see no cause to feed his own conceit or blame her forwardness. She was undoubtedly as innocent as he had always hoped he might some day find some woman.

"Don't you *love* the water?" asked Matilda, looking out at the lake as one who makes conversation after a pause too long to be quite comfortable; and Marcus, roused from his meditations, turned and looked at her. Why not then and now? It was, as Matilda had suggested, a lovely, heart-opening day, and it seemed to him—it might have been merely the languor of the sunshine—but it did seem to him that Matilda's soft blue eyes dwelt on him a little lingeringly, awaiting his reply. "Don't you love — *something?*" she had asked; he couldn't exactly remember what, but that was unimportant. Whatever it was, an obvious reply seemed so simple and possible that it was really ridiculous to omit making it. Marcus felt his heart beating faster and faster. His resolution seized him.

"No," he cried, suddenly, "but I—"

"Oh, wait—wait a minute," interrupted Matilda, in a burst of laughter. "That just reminds me of the funniest thing I heard to-day for my Address-Book. It's the story of a man who couldn't get any chance to address the girl he wanted, and so one day he got desperate, and when she happened to say, 'Don't you *love* pancakes?' He said, 'No, but I *love you.*' Isn't that a splendid one? I beg your pardon for interrupting you. I was afraid I'd forget to tell you. What were you going to say?"

"I can't remember," answered Marcus, hastily, and for the moment he thought he hated Matilda and everything concerning her, and above all the Address-Book. But he was mistaken, for this was only the beginning of a long discipline.

The day after the meeting at the lodge Marcus had supposed that he would wake to laugh at himself for a brief folly, but to his dismay what he did awake to realize was that he had become inextricably interested in a maiden whom no one but himself had discovered as

attractive at all. The vaseline had done its
work, and, as Matilda kept her promise not to
repeat her experiment, there was no repetition
of her one brief evening of triumph. Thus
Marcus had the field to himself, but his empty field was not to be easily won. In the first
place, the kind and unsuspicious friends who
were his hosts were continually rescuing him
whenever they found him, as they thought,
stranded by his good-nature on the shores of
Matilda's society. Least of all did Matilda
realize that she was an object of interest to
him. She also was constantly opening to him
avenues of escape from her side, where in her
humility it never seemed to occur to her any
one could have possibly schemed to arrive, or,
arriving, desire to stay. Marcus felt that his
whole salvation lay in the lodge set in the
lagoon, where he now considered he had first
met Matilda. Here, as often as he dared, he
followed her, escaping from his friends on the
old pretext of a love of solitary fishing. He
was not anxious to arouse the suspicions of
others, but he found that his greatest stum-
bling-block lay in the fact that, try as he might,
seek her as he would, he could not arouse the
suspicions of Matilda. He soon saw unfort-
unately well that he must make a set speech

of some kind, if he ever hoped to arouse her
to a sense of his feeling towards her, but the
circumstances were such as to make such an
effort wellnigh impossible for him.

Every time when he succeeded in leading
the conversation towards the subject nearest
his heart, Matilda would herself grasp his carefully prepared opening and take it away from
him, using it as an opportunity to talk to him
of the one thing that held him most apart from
her — the Address - Book. Marcus felt bitterly that he could never endure repeating, as he
once so nearly had repeated some one of these
odious addresses that Matilda held collected;
yet no entreaty of his ever moved her to yield
to him the book that he might read it for himself, and once for all learn what *not* to say.
Thus, while there were times when he literally
writhed under the infliction of extracts read
to him, there were other times when he listened hungrily for any crumbs of the book's
contents, ever divided between supreme thank-
fulness that he was spared another repetition
and disgust that his tongue was again tied.

There was, however, one point in which Marcus found great comfort. Matilda still continued to blush whenever she read a serious address to him, but, blushing, she still continued

to read. Evidently, though the subject caused
her some discomfort in connection with him,
it was not displeasing to her—nay, it seemed
to have a certain fascination.

This was the point of progress, or lack of
progress, at which Marcus had arrived in his
suit when that occurred which we have record-
ed at the opening of this story. And it surely
is not hard to see, with this history given, why
he felt that the worst possible contingency had
arisen when he looked up to see Matilda in her
canoe approaching his solitary and peculiar
prison.   ,

"What in the world are you standing on?"
were Matilda's first practical words, and though
in the past Marcus had sometimes felt that she
rather lacked a proper sense of humor, now
he loved her the more ardently for that defi-
ciency.

"I'm not very sure as to what I am standing
on," Marcus answered, with an effort at pleas-
antry. "I think it's a rock ; but whatever it
is, I shall always hereafter swear that I never
did stand on it, and I shall expect you to en-
dorse my falsehood as a kind of a family reparation. It was, I am sorry to say, your own
brothers who put me off their sail-boat and
deliberately left me here in this plight."

He was trying to speak easily and playfully, and really felt that he succeeded in a remarkable degree.

"Joseph and Robert!" repeated Matilda, in a bewildered way. "I just met them going home in their sail-boat, and they never said a word about you. But then they did know I was on my way here, for I told them at breakfast I was going to the lodge this morning."

Marcus turned and looked behind him. In his excitement and confusion he had not noticed that his marooning had taken place in the mouth of the lagoon that led to Matilda's lodge. Matilda went on, in distress:

"Joseph and Robert! I am so mortified! But we'll talk about that afterwards. The thing to do now is to get you off the rock. I honestly hope father 'll thrash both the boys well. But how are we going to get you off? My canoe only holds one. Wait! I know! Now don't you worry, and do just as I tell you. I was going to crochet some cord-lace this morning, and here's the ball of cord. You take it and I'll tie the end to my canoe, and you play it out as I paddle ashore. Then you can pull the canoe back to you and get in. Be careful not to upset it. But the water seems so shallow above the rock you'd be safe if you did upset."

"'WHAT IN THE WORLD ARE YOU STANDING ON?'"

As he listened, Marcus knew more surely than ever that this was the one woman in the world for him. She had not once even had a smile to repress, and her lack of humor, her domestic habits, her softness of heart, which at that moment seemed positively maternal, all tenderly appealed to him as so many comforting and exquisite virtues. He felt his heart glow as his devotion mounted, and he knew that nothing but the stern facts of his situation prevented his then and there flinging himself at her feet, despite any Address-Book on earth. As it was, he contented himself with holding fast the line that bound him to Matilda and Matilda's canoe, as she paddled hastily to the lodge wharf, carrying out her share of the programme. Marcus had then only to pull the cord and drag the empty bark back to him, to carefully step into it, and to paddle himself to the wharf. During that brief voyage his manly resolution was taken. The Address-Book still intruded itself upon his thoughts, but he made up his mind that this episode should end his silence, and this resolution grew the more fixed when Matilda met him at the wharf with the same softened look of apologetic gravity she had worn from the first.

"I'm awfully sorry the boys are so bad," she

said, as she led Marcus into the lodge. "I'm dreadfully mortified, and so will father be. Come in and dry yourself a little. I've lighted a fire on the hearth for you."

Marcus, his thoughts far enough away from the boys or a little damp clothing, took the seat by the fire which Matilda gently urged upon him, and while she considerately withdrew to the window, he made that toilet which Joseph had thoughtfully arranged for him to be able to make. He was thinking he would plunge headlong into his subject, not deciding what to say, but letting his language command him rather than he his language, when Matilda, tracing his silent gravity to displeasure, began, self-reproachfully :

"I ought to have told father before this could happen. That's really what I ought to have done. Don't you remember I did try to warn you some days ago? I knew the boys were hatching some dreadful mischief against you. Whenever they begin to call any one by one of their horrid nicknames, I always know they are plotting something very bad against that person."

Marcus turned inquiringly.

"Nickname? You didn't tell me anything about a nickname. I supposed from what you

said they'd taken a boy's spite against me for
some unknown reason. That's why I went
sailing with them to-day when they asked me.
What was the nickname?"

"I don't like to tell you," said Matilda, blushing, "because it sounds so horrid. I don't at all
know what they meant by it, and they wouldn't
tell me. Perhaps I'd better tell you now, for
you may know. For weeks they've been calling
you nothing but 'The Weasel.' 'The Weasel!'
It does sound horrid, doesn't it?"

"The *Weasel*," repeated Marcus, wonderingly. "I can't imagine—" but the next moment
the blood rushed to his forehead and he stooped
quickly over his shoes, which he had removed
as a necklace and was then drawing on his
feet. He knew now what was the familiar
air the boys had mockingly sung at him in
their retreat. The words and the air came
to him together, and in an instant the whole
abominable and ingenious plot, of which he was
intended to become the willing or unwilling
victim, unrolled before him. And how brilliantly successful they had almost been! It seemed
to him now impossible, utterly impossible, to
fall in line and play the puppet rôle consigned
to him by these young reprobates, however
acceptable that rôle might be. But a moment

before, the dénouement had seemed to Marcus almost too near. Now he felt it was further off than ever. He sat so long looking gloomily into the fire before him that Matilda at last turned away with a timid sigh and with an effort to considerately withdraw, leaving her guest to digest the animus which she could not blame him for nourishing against herself and her family. As she passed the table in the corner of the room she took up a book, and with that in her hand sat down by the window to read. As he glanced after Matilda to see this last stroke of fate, it seemed to Marcus that it was useless to struggle longer. She was reading the Address-Book.

"I am very sorry," said a timid voice from the window, breaking a dreary silence. "I hoped they were going to sail out again, but they are not; they are coming up to the wharf. You don't want to see the boys yet, do you? Oh, Mr. Garrett, I wish you could forgive us, but I can see why you won't. Wouldn't you be willing to play a little trick on the boys? If you'll hide behind that screen in the corner, I'll tell them I never saw you, and perhaps they'll think you were drowned. That would serve them right."

A desperate hope darted through the brain

of Marcus Garrett, and in answer to its suggestion he rose hurriedly. With no time for reply
to Matilda, he darted behind the screen she
pointed out just as the two breathless boys
first peered in at the door and then burst into
the lodge, looking eagerly about them.

"There she is!" cried Robert. Joseph came
towards his sister eagerly.

"Say, Matilda, did the Weasel pop?"

Matilda had half risen to her feet, her lips
had been opened to speak, but now they closed
again, and she sank back paralyzed.

"I don't know what you mean," she whispered, so weakly that her oldest brother roared
with Homeric laughter as response.

"My, ain't she innocent! And been meeting him right here all summer long! We
haven't got a sail-boat for nothin'. Don't know
why we called him Weasel either, do you? Say,
Milly, you don't mean you went and saved his
life, and then let him go, after all the trouble
we took? Well, you are dead easy."

Robert broke in anxiously:

"Did somebody else rescue him? You don't
tell us somebody else took him off? You got
there in time, didn't you?"

Joseph answered for his speechless sister.

"Yes. There's the wet place on the floor

223

where he stood. Can't you see it for yourself?
—and there's the fire she built to dry him, and
then let him off."

"What's the use in our working for her?"
asked Robert, in deep disgust.

Matilda, after her first vain endeavor to
stem this torrent, stood gazing wildly from
one brother to the other, then sank back in
her chair, and, taking the only course left open
to her, burst into tears.

"There's gratitude for you," said Joseph,
waving his hand towards her. "Here we've
done as much and more for her than a mother
would, most stove the boat in doing it, and
now look at her! I wash my hands of you—
yes, I do. You can pop your own Weasels—
only you can't!"

"Oh!" sobbed Matilda, desperately. "Stop,
do stop! You don't know what you are doing."

"We know what we tried to do," accused
Joseph. "We tried to hurry him for you a little, and you botched the whole thing as soon
as you got hold of it. Ain't we your brothers?
I tell you he's got to live up to his name. But
how in the world can anybody help a softy like
you? And he—he must be a chump!"

At that moment the screen at the back of
the room quivered, then opened wide, and Mar-

cus walked out from behind the folds. He
looked neither to right nor to left, but walked
past the gaping boys straight to Matilda's
side.

"Matilda," he said, firmly, speaking to her
bowed head, "your brothers are entirely right.
Though how they have known so much about
us without condescending to something like
key-holes, I don't know. If you had been anybody else—but there, I wouldn't have cared for
you if you had been—you would have known
all along that the only thing which prevented
my speaking was this abominable book."

He took up the Address-Book which lay in
Matilda's lap, and with it held gingerly between his finger and thumb, walked to the
fireplace.

"You built this fire for my comfort," he said,
"and the greatest comfort it can bestow on me
is by burning this book. Matilda—Matilda!
may I burn it?"

His heart stood still as he ended, and—so
potent still was the power of the hated volume
upon him—he knew with angry certainty that
the break in his voice and his hesitation were
not caused so much by uncertainty as to what
Matilda's reply might be as by dread lest the
question he asked, which he found startingly

direct and transcribable in the asking, might yet find lodgment in the Address-Book.

"Matilda!" he called, sharply, in his distress; and Matilda, lifting a face bathed in tears, cried out in answer:

"Oh, burn, burn!—and welcome!"

Even as she spoke the Address-Book fell in the flames, and rising, as Sindbad must have risen in the moment when the Old Man of the Sea no longer burdened his back, Marcus turned from the *auto-da-fé* to discover that he was alone in the lodge with Matilda. From the wharf outside came the sound of hurrying feet and splashing water; then the echo of boyish laughter and boyish voices, singing in unison with each other, more and more distant each moment. It was the same air they had sung when they left Marcus on the rock to encounter his fate, indeed, but now the words also were plain:

> "Queen Victoria's sick abed,
> Napoleon has the measles;
> That's the way the money goes,
> And Pop *goes the Weasel.*"

Matilda and Marcus heard them not. The Address-Book was a blazing ruin in the back-

ground. Marcus had lived up to his cogno-
men, and Matilda—Matilda, contrite for past
blindness, wide-eyed for the present, and radiant for the future — was his. What more
was there to hear?

A TEMPLE OF SOLOMON

"And even your police are more sympathetic than ours. Last night I was getting home about a square at a time—I and one of the other boys—and the gendarme was polite all the way. 'Gentlemen, I must rouse you again. A thousand pardons! I beg you won't let me find you on *this* door-step when I return.' And then he'd find us on another a block along, and do the whole thing all over again. We had just a little way to go, if it did take us half the night, so it was all on his beat. I suppose they have beats something like ours, don't they?"

The listener, a man much older than his companion, looked up and nodded slightly.

"All worlds are alike," he said, smiling.

"Indeed they are not! Not like our world. Why, I can't fancy myself sitting with a metaphorical wet towel around my head and sodas at my elbow, talking of the night before to a man of your age and standing, sir, on our side of the water. Yet I know I can with you. You are all more men of the world here. You don't make me feel that you are shocked now."

" No, Mr. Delano," said the older man, good-naturedly, and nodding his head again; "I don't think I can call myself shocked."

He was looking at the boyish figure lounging with a somewhat ostentatious air of fatigue in the easy-chair. If a gleam of amusement lurked in his eyes, it was hidden in their depths. He spoke English accurately and easily, but with a marked accent and slow enunciation, and his manner to his young companion was almost deferential in its exquisite courtesy. The boy expanded under the benign influence like a flower in the sun, turning out the innermost petals.

" I like it here," young Delano went on, warmly, and with a not unpleasing egotism. " It's horribly expensive—all my money-orders are just round-trip tickets, right in and out again; but I like your methods of life, I like your ways."

" And our sympathy with a gentleman that night and the next morning ?"

" Well, I suppose most of you have had next mornings yourselves," said the youth, naïvely.

He flushed and looked up hastily as his companion suddenly laughed aloud. "I believe all Americans think that of us. How is the work going? And how do you find B—— treats you?"

"Horribly," laughed the boy. He leaned forward and spoke eagerly, rapidly, almost childishly, quite forgetting his earlier assumption of the blasé. His voice was charmingly boyish and merry.

"Why, do you know, he simply laid me out the first day. I'd been taught to draw in my work with my brush—no outlines—and that's what he found on my easel. It was a messy-looking thing. I didn't know as much as I know now, so I waited by my work to see what he'd say. He didn't say anything for some time, and then—goodness! I don't like to remember it even now! 'Humph! Starting a new school, M. Delano?' Said that so the whole room heard him! I nearly died. 'You can take a crayon and draw, draw, draw from the model each day.' I was fighting mad, but there was no one to fight."

The elder man laughed heartily.

"Just like him. He was like that in my day. I remember my first encounter with him. I was unwise, like you. I stupidly waited for his first comments. He paused so long at my easel that I couldn't stand it. I asked him, trembling, 'What's wrong, monsieur?' He waved his hand around like this, utterly despairing. 'I don't know. I give it up!' And those were my first words from him. Our profession has its rubs, comrade."

Young Delano flushed gratefully, but with a nice sense of shame.

"I almost wish you wouldn't talk to me in that way, sir," he burst out. "When you speak with that kind of manner of equality I feel as small as a pin. You are so immeasurably above me—I mean, above anything I might ever hope to be. I mean—it makes me blush and stammer like this to think of any presumption of comradeship with you, Monsieur R——"

The name he spoke was that of an artist in whose work nations delighted. Despite his boyish enthusiasm of protests, the young host did not, and could not, fully realize the honor done him in the mere presence in his room of this genius. A formal card of introduction given to Delano by his father had presented him to Monsieur R——, and this was not, it seemed to him, reason sufficient to account for occasional visits and unobtrusive but unwavering kindness from so great a source. In his heart he decided that some quality in his own work had caught these critical eyes. If, then, with so little effort he had interested this critic, what might he not do when he put forth his powers? He meant to get down to work in earnest so soon as he had seen a little more of life—a little more of this enchanting capital of high art and light living. At his guest's request he drew out, with no hesitation, whatever work he had finished, and listened respectfully, as he always listened, to the gentle, subtle, but praiseless criticisms.

"I can never tell you how kind I think this is of you," Delano said, easily; "but of course you must have known, without my telling you, how your interest in my art encourages me."

Monsieur R—— looked up serenely from the sketch he held in his hand. "My dear boy," he said, emotionlessly, "your art doesn't interest me. It would be wrong for me to let you think that. *You* interest me immensely, your art not at all."

The words were so courteously, so gently said that their great importance seemed denied by the manner of their utterance; yet Delano stood gasping as if ice-water had been cruelly flung in his smiling face. Monsieur R—— glanced up again at him and rose immediately.

" You must pardon me," he said, regretfully.
"I did not realize. Is art, then, so dear to you?"

Delano hated the weakness in his throat that
made his voice come huskily. "If I didn't love
art, why am I here?"

The artist shook his head with a mournful
half-smile and slight shrug. "All who are
here do not love art."

Delano walked quickly past him to the table,
and laid his hand unsteadily on the sketches
he had spread out there. "You said just now
it would be wrong for you to let me think you
found interest in my work," he said, proudly.
"As I have been thinking just that, will you
tell me why you have chosen to be kind to
me?"

The older man raised his eyes and looked at
the boy whose self-respect he had wounded
with a long, slow gaze, neither too searching
nor too slighting.

"I am sorry," he said, simply. "I am sorry
I spoke so brutally, but you will find that every
Gaul ceases to possess that civility you say you
admire the moment art is in question. Let me
say one more word of your work, as I have said
thus much. There is nothing here for me to
talk of seriously."

He laid his long, slim hand on the pictures,

233

and, his courtly gentleness thrown abruptly aside, spoke with a fire and power the boy had never seen in him before. "These are very fair, all good enough. Some have a certain power in them; all have some promise, all are clever, but *you* didn't paint these. Your head and your hands did; but how small a part of a man are his head and hands! Art, believe me, art is a vampire—no less. Its very existence demands life-blood, heart-blood. I can only tell you that there is no trace, not a trace, of such carmine in any of all this work. Whether it suffers by your fault or your misfortune is for you to decide. You, and you alone, can know what you have suffered in the effort to put yourself in your work. But this is enough. Pardon me. I don't come here to preach platitudes to you. I came to be amusing. That question you last asked lets me be somewhat amusing, perhaps. You asked why I am interested in you. This room has something to do with that interest. It was once occupied by a man with a story. And, by-the-way, did you know that your father, too, lived in this room when he was in Paris?"

"Yes, I knew it," said Delano, briefly. His voice came from close behind his teeth. He was striving with himself to reply at all. " Per-

234

haps," he exclaimed, bitterly, "I am only a dabbler by birthright. I know I haven't worked; but why should I? What inheritance of real art and of tradition have I? We are a family of shopkeepers. I belong behind the counter, too, I suppose. I don't know where we got this infernal twist in our minds that sends us to Paris to make fools of ourselves—father and son. My father failed miserably over here, as you know, I suppose. He never speaks of it at home. And now here am I."

"Your father," said Monsieur R——, interrupting gently, "never made a fool of himself for a moment. When he found out that his path in life was not to be art, he went home quietly and soberly. He was in some of the same classes that I was in, and I have never known any man, before or since, whom I respected so thoroughly, except, perhaps, the occupant of this same room whose story I wanted to tell you. Would you care to hear it?"

Delano stood dejectedly by the table, gazing at his canvases. His dark, full eyes, sensitive as a young girl's, were clouded and wet, but he looked up frankly. "It's all over now," he said, manfully. "I didn't take that criticism well, but it was unexpected to me. I'm used to Monsieur B——'s scoldings; I expect them. This was different. It's knocked the nonsense out of me. I ought to have felt for myself all of what you said, and if there were any real artist blood in me I would have felt it. I don't belong in this life any more than my father did. I shall go home, too—after I break my brushes. If I can't use them, no one else shall. Do you mind if I give them a last washing while you tell me your story? I'd like them to go to their death in decent order."

The elder man made no attempt to dissuade him or change his resolution. He began his story quietly, with his hands laid loosely on the table, while the boy sadly scrubbed his brushes round and round in the palm of his hand, cleaning them after the not very tidy manner of art students.

" Some time ago," said Monsieur R——, " a young American of about your age and circumstances came into our art classes, and, as I told you, took this same room that you and your father have had. He, like you both, was of a commercial people, but the most hopeful creature, the most confident in his own success. He had a love for art, a passion for art, that I envy him to this day. I have never seen any human love like it. I used to come to see him here constantly, and I never left him without

having learned something of him that no school
of art could teach. He worked early, he worked
late. I think he would have liked to paint with
his feet when his hands were too tired to hold
the brush, and for nature's beauties he had a
soul like an octagon, with a wide-open door at
each corner. Go to the window there a moment, and tell me what you see."

Delano, with a subdued manner cf childlike
obedience, dropped the work on his brushes and
went to the window, where he looked out.

"I can't see anything but roofs and chim-
neys and a gray sky," he said.

Monsieur R—— rose and joined him. "And
I," he said—"I see, first, a lovely pattern on
that façade of the house-roof. The snow has
fallen, filling up all the crevices of the stone ;
only the raised brown carving stands above
the soft white background. Over there, I see
a gray cloud of hovering smoke shaped like a
giant mushroom above a chimney. The air
is too heavy to spread it farther. Why didn't
you see those things? But I never did until
I was taught to see them by my brother art
student. There were in every scene some hidden charms that were lost to me until I saw
it with him, and then they were no longer hidden. What training my eyes have had, what

success is mine, is in a great degree due to the hours I have spent in this room. Do you wonder that I feel a pleasure in seeing these walls about me again?"

"No," said Delano, slowly. He came back to his brush-washing. Inch by inch it seemed to him the artist was thrusting him from him. For all reasons except for Delano's sake he had visited this room. Monsieur R—— went on with his story, leaning now against the window-frame and looking out on the snowy roofs.

"Then," he said, "there came a day—a day that was terrible. For weeks I had feared what came then. I went to the oculist with him, and I led him home. He walked like a drunken man and flung himself on that very bed where you lie every night of your thoughtless life. Just there a strong man's ambition died hard; an absorbing passion burned out in a live body; a heart broke. I sat where you are sitting, and I suffered it all as he suffered. It was the purest of ambitions. He had no need of money, no need to rise in the world, because he was contented where he was born. It was the rare and pure ambition of a noble genius, and those poor little doors at which it was creeping out into our world were slowly and cruelly closing it in forever. He would see well enough to lead an ordinary life—no more. I sat there and watched him for an hour. He was to have no pain to suffer. He was not suffering pain then, but it was an hour's death-agony I witnessed. Then he got up from the bed and walked steadily to that desk over there, and I knew it was to write the home letter. He had taken up the new life, and this was its first work. He picked up a letter which he found lying on the desk, addressed to him, and opened it with evident bewilderment. It had neither stamp nor postmark. I had laid it there when we first came into the room. Presently he came to me and laid his hand on my shoulder. 'Read this,' he said, clearly, and there was a triumph in his voice that for me rings in this room yet. I read the letter, and I begged for it to keep as a talisman. I needed it more than he ; his life was planned for him, mine was all to live. This has helped me through the rains ; it has helped me in the sunshines of my life. It has made me more an artist, more a man, than I could ever have been without it. I read it myself constantly, and, as you see by its worn edges I always carry it ; and now I am going to read it to you. It begins, 'My dear Son,' and it is signed, 'Your Father':

A TEMPLE OF SOLOMON

"MY DEAR SON,—Your friend, Monsieur R——, has some weeks ago written to me that he feared your eyesight was in danger, though you did not suspect it, and he kindly begged me to prepare myself for the worst, and also to spare you the pain of writing this news to me. I therefore send you this letter by him, and when you receive it you will know that you have nothing to tell me. I am not quite sure how this trouble will find you, but if you are without consolation you must remember that it's all in a lifetime, and life is not long. But somehow I turn to the thought that you will not let this crush you. I want you the same boy that I never understood, but that I have loved—as his father loved Benjamin—more than all my other boys. You were never under my hand as the others were. When I thought I had you, it was like catching a bird under my fingers—a leg out, a wing out, a head out—you were gone. You escaped me in spirit always, and I want you to do so still. Some must be the foundation-stones and some the spires. We can't all shoot upward. Whenever I saw you fail and set your teeth and drudge until you got the idea you worked for, I used to say to myself, "That's his daddy." I couldn't paint, no indeed, but I knew I was the old foundation-stone that had given you the power to drudge and drudge, and so to climb, and you could never shoot up very far without that as a foothold under you. It was a great joy for me to feel this—a great joy—and yours will be a doubled joy if you can look at your son's work and say, "I was the stone that lifted him up far higher than my father lifted me, for I gave him both genius and the power to drudge."

"'Come home, my boy, and drudge and dream, and dream and drudge, and make all you can of what you have left to you, and then pass it on. We shall live, or you will, to send out a third generation, with all our best powers stored in him. You and I must be like the pieces of the temple of Solomon when it lay all apart and separate, only waiting to be put together. When we are united in your son, it shall be a fair temple of high spires, please God. He shall have the power to dream such dreams as *you* have dreamed, and to work as *I* have worked. Come home; the old beehive is big enough to keep us both busy, and, my boy—will it hurt you for me to say this?—your work isn't needed of the world. It is God's work to paint as you paint, but God will take care of his own work, and it is not for you to worry that you are not looking after it. Come home and look after me. I am growing old. Marry, and give me a grandson, and we shall yet be famous. Take courage, if you have ever lost courage; but the man who believes you have not is   YOUR FATHER.'"

There was a long pause. Delano had ceased washing his brushes. He was listening intently.

"Would you like to see the letter?" asked Monsieur R——. He laid it on the table before the boy and turned away again to the window.

As Delano glanced down at the writing, he started; then, turning the pages quickly, looked for a moment incredulously at the printed heading. He laid the letter down on the table, and, rising suddenly, set his hand on it, palm down, with a gesture as of a man planting his foot firmly on the lowest rung of life's ladder.

"Why didn't you—why didn't they tell me this before?" he cried, angrily. "What a fool—what a fool I have been !"

Monsieur R—— looked at the flushed face keenly. "You were not ready before," he said, gently ; "but now—yes, you are the son of your father and grandfather, and they 'shall yet be famous.'"

THIS MORTAL COIL

Long ago, in æons past, Nature, kneading an iron shore to suit her mood, twisted off a great careless lump of red rock and flung it into the ocean ; then, as if by an after-thought, she tied it to dry land with a rope of knotted bowlders. Thus created, Brace's Rock has stood for centuries in the blue waters, naked at first, but slowly clothing itself with a spare growth of golden-rod in its crevices, some stunted bay-bushes, and starved feathery grass.

There the gaunt rock stood on a certain September afternoon, the sweeping sea-line spread out before its face, while at its back, in a pond-like shelter, gathered hundreds of sea-gulls, looking like pads of white pond-lilies on the still cove's waters, or, yet more lovely, flaunting and fluttering their white wings as, perched on the little brown rock islands, they fought the waves of the rising tide, white-tipped as they. In all Septembers this shore revels in colors that shade back from the gray sand-beach and the spring green of the sand-grass to moors warm and rich with color that seems to fairly dash up the sides of the gray-peaked inland rocks, splashing high among them red-leaved bushes and mats of glowing brown or purple pink grasses.

Lawrence Goodhue, on this September day, sat on the topmost ledge of Brace's Rock, his elbow on his knee, his chin in his hand, his artist eyes garnering the scene into the store-house of his brain, and so absorbed was he in details of color that when at last his gaze dropped to a spot not ten feet from him he sat staring at it with a sense of confusion. What he saw was an artist's paint-rag, still wet and fresh with all the shaded colors of the land-scape, but for the moment it was to him al-most as if his vision had collected the wide-spread colors, as a prism might, and thrown them together on the rock.

Sending his eyes wandering again in search of the fellow-artist who must have preceded him, Goodhue finally discovered a figure climbing among the rocks below. It was plainly a woman, though as he peered down at her a large, mush-room-like hat concealed from him everything but a white skirt and an identifying artist's equipment hanging from the climber's shoulder.

244

Not an hour before, Goodhue had been over every inch of that lower ground, and he now watched the progress of another with peculiar interest. At what he felt to be the risk of life and limb, he had crawled down not only to the base of the rock itself, but under a jutting bowlder overhanging the water, and there discovered a veritable jewel-casket. The waters, lapping in and out twice daily between the crevices, had formed somehow a great oblong basin, and this the sea had filled with its own wonders. It had first draped the gray sides with long, weeping sea-weeds, or crusted them with tawny barnacles and black mussels dashed with silver. There spongy anemones of every soft tint stretched down thirsty necks, while the floor below was a rich mosaic formed of multi-colored snails, with here a blazing orange starfish, there another of pink or royal purple. The approach to this treasure-house lay down a sharp descent, slippery with wet weeds and black with barnacles, and it was a recollection of the difficulties of the climb, not unwillingness to see another share his discovery, that brought Goodhue to his feet and made him look down anxiously as the stranger artist paused above the overhanging rock. He realized that she too had found some evidence of what lay below as he watched her hesitate, test with her foot the slippery weed on the rocks, then draw back, only to repeat the attempt at another point. Foiled, apparently, by the real dangers of the descent, she seated herself at last on an overhanging rock, as Goodhue thought wisely giving up the attempt. He fancied that a sketch of the pool was to be the next move in order, as he saw the girl take what looked like a sketch-book from her side, but by a deliberate movement she poised the book with careful aim and flung it swiftly down under the rock ; then, with only a moment's hesitation, she rose, plunged after it, and was lost to Goodhue's astonished sight. Although he had found the descent difficult as well as dangerous, he remembered that both difficulty and danger had been doubled in the return, and deciding, therefore, that he should at least be near at hand in the event of accident, he made his way quickly down the side of the rock, and, reaching the top of the overhanging spur, waited there patiently. It amused him, unseen and unsuspected as he knew he was, and knowing as he did every beauty that lay in that hidden aquarium of nature, to hear now and then half-uttered exclamations of delight coming from beneath the rock. It was long, and he did not wonder at the delay, before the sound of a foot cautiously scraping its way warned him that the reckless adventurer, having satisfied her artistic curiosity, had finally begun her ascent. He moved softly nearer to the jagged edge, and a moment later saw a woman's un-gloved hand groping helplessly in air ; but before Goodhue had decided whether he should or should not grasp it, the hand was clinging to a blunt projection, where the companion hand soon followed, creeping about the other side of the blunt spur. Small and white as they were, the hands seemed supple and the wrists so strong that Goodhue waited to discover what plan their owner had for them before he inter-fered. Stooping down and crawling to the rock's edge, he looked cautiously over to see that the climber was standing on the narrowest of ledges, with her body thrown back to gain the impetus which was to swing her about the rough corner, using the spur as a pivot, her arms as ropes to drag her up to the top of the rock. There was no time for further hesita-tion. Goodhue grasped the girl's wrists, at the same time crying out a warning.

"Don't jump ! It is dangerous. Have you kept your footing ?"

" Yes," answered a voice from below.

He braced himself against the rock. " Then swing free now and I'll pull you up. Slowly! Slowly!" He felt the muscles of her wrists relax as her hands loosened on the spur and the weight of her body hung on his arms. In another moment he knew she must have gained some new footing, for the strain on his hands lifted in part, and the next instant the mushroom hat was rising over the rock's edge, disclosing to his interested eyes, first a cloud of dark hair, next the white brow it surrounded, and then his eyes met those heavy-lashed blue eyes unlike any others he had ever known. Had the overhanging rock on which he knelt dropped into the pool beneath, it seemed to Goodhue that the crash could not have been more actual than was this meeting eye to eye. A moment, still poised as they were, both were held motionless, then, with a word of inarticulate exclamation, Goodhue dragged the girl's limp body up the face of the rock to the spot where he stood. With solid ground beneath her feet, her first motion was to stagger from Goodhue's support and lean weakly against the stone wall which rose high above them. But if her body was weak her fixed eyes could still ask the question her lips were unable to demand, and with an effort Goodhue answered her exactly as if she had spoken.

"Hester, on my honor, I did not know it was you! Your hat hid your face. I came to help you only as any man would go to any woman in danger."

Hester drew her trembling figure together against the rough rock to which she seemed to cling. Though she spoke, it was as if the wind caught her voice, blowing it from her lips, it came so faintly, so unnaturally.

"Not—not this man to this woman!"

"No," he replied, sadly, "you are right. We should never have met again; but indeed if one of these waves had caught us off the land somewhere and flung us together on this rock, our meeting could not have been more accidental."

"I believe you, and if I had had a moment of preparation"—she looked up at him, fully and proudly meeting his eyes—"I could have met you as any woman might meet any man."

As she ended she bent her head slightly and, crossing the small rocky platform, quickly disappeared behind the first jutting rock. Before he realized that she was going, Goodhue found himself alone, but the little sketch-book, which he had seen her fling under the rock, lay where she had dropped it, forgotten, at his feet. Goodhue stooped and lifted the book. He hesitated a moment with it in his hand, then passed round the rock where Hester had vanished. As she heard his quick step she turned instantly with a look as if at bay, resolute, yet needing all her resolution. Goodhue at once held out the book towards her, advancing no farther than it was needful to do so.

"I doubted whether I ought to follow you with it," he said, constrainedly. "I saw you fling this away—but then I also saw you risk your life to recover it. I did not know—"

"I should have been sorry to lose it. I flung it away only because I was afraid to climb down under the rock; but I knew I should have to go down after the book was there. Thank you for bringing it to me. I should have thanked you also for your assistance, and I do now."

If they had never met before, her manner would have been perfect, keeping him at his distance, sufficiently grateful and explanatory and very simple; yet had they never met there could not have been in her eyes the veiled contempt he too plainly read there. As she ended it was as if she dismissed him, but though she held out her hand for the book, Goodhue did not give it to her. He was standing motionless, looking in her face so closely that despite her self-control her color rose slowly and hotly. As he saw it mounting to her throat, her cheek, her brow, he spoke, slowly :

"Hester, can't you forgive me?"

For a moment she did not reply, then answered, with effort, "I had forgiven you—until I saw you."

"I understand. I am going now. But one word, one moment first. It was, believe me, for your sake more than for my own that I acted as I did. I know you cannot judge, not knowing what I do."

She turned to him suddenly, hotly. "I can know that I am profoundly grateful to you for what you saved me from. I know now it would have been a living death to me. You saved me from that, and for that favor—but how can you think I should ever wish to see your face again?"

"I do not," he answered, gravely. "I am going now. But remember, I know nothing, I have heard not a word since we parted—not even that I spared you all I could. I told your father that you found the man of my letters, the man you had promised yourself to, not at all the man I was. Was it accepted?"

"If it gives you any comfort, it was accepted. You generously gave me the honors of war and I accepted them. But why should I play out the part with you, who know those honors were thrust upon me!"

Goodhue stood with bowed head, repudiating nothing. He half turned away, then looked back. "Before I go," he said, simply, "you need not prepare for what I am going to say. It seems very prosaic to mention this at all, but let me warn you, as I crossed the causeway from the main-land to this rock, I noticed the bowlders scattered on the causeway were wave worn. This, with some other signs, made me sure that at high tide, whenever that may be, this rock would be cut off."

"Submerged?"

"Hardly," he answered, glancing with a smile at the craggy heights above. "A rise of tide that submerged this rock would flood all the main-land as well, but the causeway is much lower."

Hester glanced back at the water behind them. At that moment a wave, stronger than its fellows, swelled up and broke on the outer rocks, rushing over their serrated tops as though so many gateways, flooding the plat-form where they had stood a few moments before, and sobbing up almost to their feet in a trough of dashing spray and foam. The seaweed clinging to the rocks was no longer a flat drapery, the waves were lifting their drooping heads on strong crests to toss and tangle them roughly.

Hester started as she looked. "The tide is rising!"

"Yes," Goodhue answered, "it has been rising for some time. I am afraid high tide cannot be far off. It would really be wiser to make your escape good at once. The quickest way is up over the centre of the rock, only it is very steep. If you would let me help you "— he hesitated, but Hester hurriedly took the hand he had half offered, and breathlessly toiled after him on the steep ascent which they at once began. In many places Goodhue had almost to drag her up the rock's sheer face, as he had done on their meeting at its base. There was no chance for speech even had either desired it. Hester climbed with a feverish haste, and Goodhue, yielding to her mood, hurried the ascent as rapidly as he dared. Once, as he touched her arm to aid her, he felt that her whole body was trembling, and he looked up at her quickly.

"Are you afraid?" he asked. "I assure you

there's no possibility of danger. Even if the tide has covered the causeway, the worst that can happen will be a short imprisonment. This rock could not possibly be submerged."

She glanced at him a moment and then turned away again, pressing forward faster. "Perhaps," she said, coldly, "I might prefer submersion."

Goodhue colored and drew back. "I beg your pardon—" he began.

But at that moment they reached the summit, which gave them the first glimpse of the causeway, last seen as a ridge of red rock strewn with bowlders and bounded on either side by the sea. Now between them and dry land lay a stretch of unquiet waters flecked with little wave-worn islands, some as close together as easy stepping-stones over a brook, but others more dubiously distant. Even as they looked the rising waves, swimming in from the sea, were swallowing up these means of escape as rapidly as fishes devour crumbs of bread.

Goodhue turned to look at his companion. They had both paused abruptly.

"I shall attempt it," Hester said, decidedly, in answer to his look, and at once began the descent, much easier on this side than the ascent on the other. Goodhue was at her side when she reached the beach that lay at the foot of the rock, but she seemed almost unconscious of his presence. As she stood poised lightly on a stone at the water's edge, her eager blue eyes on the farther shore, her face flushed, her lips set, her dark hair blown back, her whole figure as a type of motion, but for the moment arrested, it seemed to Goodhue as great an impertinence to suggest danger to her as it would be to suggest it to the sea-gulls fluttering on the outlying rocks, disputing their possession with the buffeting waves that constantly swept them aside. Yet, when she lifted her foot from the first rock to set it on the next, he quickly stepped forward and laid his hand on her arm, half speaking his thought:

"But you have no wings. It is impossible."

Her impatient movement was meant to shake off his detaining hand. "There is nothing to prevent my trying."

His hand still on her arm, he felt the forward spring of her body, and again deliberately resisted it, pushing her back. Her foot dropped to the sand.

"You forget me," he said, gently. "I must prevent your trying it."

"You prevent me!" she asked, incredulously. "You mean to keep me here by force?"

He answered her urgently. "You surely will not make me do that. You must see the danger. Willing as I am to help you escape, I cannot, you cannot measure from here the distances of those bowlders from each other, nor the depths between them. You might be caught midway, with retreat or advance cut off and the tide still rushing in. Then any fall for you among those sharp stones and angry waters could have but one end."

"You are afraid."

He looked at her with a half smile. "Yes," he said, "I am afraid. Did you think you could scourge me to courage?"

Her eyes lowered, she stood silent for the moment, then suddenly, with hands clasped, raised her eyes in entreaty. "I implore you to let me try it. I am very strong. I sha'n't be hurt. You must see I can't—I can't stand staying here."

"I do see that, and I don't mean you shall stay here—with me. The only thing I do beg of you is not to attempt the passage until the way is quite clear again. You won't be imprisoned very long at worst."

Goodhue was taking off his coat as he ended, and Hester stood looking at him in silence, her face changing. As he rolled his coat into a

256

bundle and thrust it under his arm, she spoke coldly and abruptly:

"You called the passage very dangerous just now. If that is true, I cannot allow you to attempt it. If anything should happen, my conscience—"

He interrupted her quickly. "I thank your conscience—but it may rest easy. I am a strong swimmer. In any case I go solely on my own responsibility." A bitterness that for the first time spoke in his voice brought the color to Hester's face.

"I did not mean to be unkind," she said, still formally, but more gently than she had yet spoken. "I only meant that I could not let you risk your life to spare me mere discomfort."

"Yes," he answered, sadly. "I understood you. You meant what you said. It was a case of conscience only. Good-bye, I don't ask you to reply. You were right. We should never have met, and now we must part as quickly as possible. Good-bye."

Before she could speak again, had she wished to do so, he had left her side, and was leaping from rock to rock out into the waters. Hester turned sharply away back to the higher sand of the beach. There, where they had stood in

the sand, together in all human probability
for the last time, she saw the marks of Goodhue's footsteps and her own distinctly printed.
The ripples that left the rushing waves behind
to break on the sand in wrinkles soft as a baby's
frown were yet strong enough to be wiping
out these last frail memorials. Hester's brow
contracted as she looked, but she moved resolutely on with no backward glance, until a little bird, darting with a sharp chirp from some
crevice, flew past her, almost brushing her with
its wings in its hurry to be off. Turning involuntarily to watch its dipping flight, her eyes
caught a glimpse of Goodhue's figure standing
on a rock far out in the yeasty waters.

Brace's heights rose solidly between her and
the inland when she stopped again and stood
looking out at the distant sea-line. The sun,
now almost level with the world, was behind
the rock, and cast the shadows of its peaks in
longer and longer reflections at her feet. The
deserted waste of waters lay cold and gray.
Two finger-like light-houses on a distant island
were pointing upward, their straight lines already blurring and purpling in the withdrawing light. The air seemed suddenly cold, and
Hester shivered involuntarily. As if seeking
for warmth, she nestled down in one of the

rock crevices, leaning close against the stone's rough side as she waited, watching the waves that came dashing in, throwing their spray almost to her feet. The roaring of the waves was so monotonous and continuous she heard nothing, until at last, at a step close behind her, she turned with a start to see Goodhue.

"You have not gone?" she cried, rising and facing him.

"You must not blame me," he answered. "After all, it proved impossible."

"The tide had risen too high?"

He paused a moment, then replied, with grave significance: "Yes, the tide had risen too high. I might play with words and still say that too truly. But I have come back solely because I love you and because I must tell you so."

She stood staring at him bewildered, and he repeated his last words.

"I must tell you so."

"No," she cried, rousing. "You could have left me, and have dared to come back for this! How have you ventured? Do you think you can once fling a woman's heart away and ever come back—"

He checked her with an earnest gesture. "Flung away! And you have thought there

259

was no better reason than that kind of faith-lessness? Then, indeed, you must hear me."

"Never. Never again!"

"You must. In justice to me, first you must listen, and, further — as you yourself decide. For a year I have let you judge me unheard, because I could not speak. Now I can, and claim a hearing. In common justice, you have no right to refuse." .

"I do refuse. In common justice, I have some claims. I did love you. You know it. Why should I deny it?" She caught her breath for the moment, but went on. "I have at last reached the point I made up my mind I would reach the day we parted. I don't deny it was hard at first, but I have utterly ceased to care. I will not be troubled now. I have the right not to be."

He stood looking at her face, flushed and quivering, but decided—at the indignant violet eyes which she forced herself to raise to his, and at the curve of her quivering lips. Then he looked away from her again out over the waters about them.

"We are as if in a world quite apart for the time," he said, at last, quaintly. "I wish we could forget for these few moments that there's any other world to consider. When

260

our souls meet in another world they will perhaps talk of all this freely together. Why shouldn't we speak now, as it may be we shall speak then? Our friends know nothing of this meeting—they need never know. All that is in our own hands. When we leave this little island for the earth again, you could take the path to the left, I to the right, and, if you so will it, all can be as if this talk had never been."

He turned towards her again, speaking less resolutely, more earnestly: "Can't you give me out of your whole lifetime these few moments—in this place so far out of the world? A few moments is all I ask."

Hester stood looking away from him at the ever-strengthening waves. Once she turned and glanced at him, and he saw she hesitated, but he would not urge her.

"If I could be sure," she began, slowly—"if I could be sure that the earthly would not enter—"

He interrupted her quickly. "In your hardest thoughts of me, have you ever accused me of deceiving you?"

"Not of deception."

"Then accept my promise. If you consent the earthly shall not enter."

She looked up at him again, and as he met her look fully and gravely, she turned as if to find a seat on the shelving rock behind them. Goodhue accepted the implied consent.

"But we shouldn't stop here," he said, practically. "The sun is so low on the other side of the rock, this side is growing too cold. If we climb to the top of the rock we can catch the warmth of the last rays, and we can watch the causeway, too, as it uncovers."

Hester let him help her to the heights, and sat down silently in the crevice he selected as yielding most comfort for her. Goodhue knew she was waiting for him to speak, but he was silent, looking down towards the causeway wiped wholly out of existence by the sea.

"The tide is full, I think," he said, finally. "We have only to wait for it to fall."

Hester's eyes also were fixed in the distance, he believed on nothing.

Goodhue spoke abruptly. "Perhaps it will be easier to plunge in at once. When we parted, had you no idea of what parted us? Did you never"—his gaze dropped to her hands which lay clasped in her lap—"suspect another woman?" He saw her fingers tighten suddenly, and, glancing up, saw her quivering face, and bent towards her with a word of protest on his lips; but before it found utterance she had moved back, still facing him and meeting his eyes so fully and collectedly that he caught his breath.

"Go on," she answered, simply. "It was the first cut only that hurt. I had suspected this among other things. Have you more to say?"

"Something I scarcely dare put into words. Do you remember nothing strange in our first letters?"

"Nothing," she answered, after a moment's thought.

"Because you have not the key yet. When I first wrote you from my Paris studio, you remember it was about some unimportant detail of color which we had discussed together. You recollect that?"

"Yes, and I replied, thanking you. It all seemed unimportant."

"Yet you couldn't know how your reply, short as it was, differed from anything I expected. There was nothing very marked in it, yet it was different. Later, when I had drawn another and another letter from you, I did write you that I had scarcely dared hope for any answers whatever, because when we met you seemed so shy and inaccessible. A wood

263

violet could not have been more retiring. Did you never wonder at my thinking that?"

"Why should I? You had met me in a crowded house-party for two days only. That was all. I saw you had gained a wrong impression of me, which I remember I attempted to dispel."

"It was done quickly and effectively, and forever. For days I did not know whether your letter of self-revelation most fascinated me or bewildered me. It was all so truthful, so delicate, so fantastic, yet so unlike my idea of what you were. First you condoled with me teasingly as a color-blind artist mistaking a rose for a violet. Then you went on more seriously to tell me there were rose-women and violet-women born into the world differing as distinctly as the flowers, and the perfume of the rose was not the perfume of the violet. That was all, but it was enough to reveal you. Hester, when I laid your letter down, I could smell roses! Later, perhaps then, I knew I loved you, and when at last I wrote you so, you answered—you know what you answered." He paused and went on with difficulty, but rapidly, not looking at her. "I could hardly wait to finish my work—hardly wait to cross to you—and then I stood in your home waiting for you to come down to me, and I could call up, as I think only an artist can, every feature of the woman I had seen but once and learned to love by letter only—remember that. How shall I tell you? Your eyes are violet, your hair is dark. The face I saw so vividly as I waited there for you had soft brown eyes and the hair was fair, and—it was Anne's face I saw, Hester."

"Anne—my own sister. Oh no—no! She has been with me night and day through all this—she could not—"

"She knew nothing—knows nothing now."

"Oh, speak plainly—my own sister!"

Goodhue laid his hands strongly on hers as they lay trembling on her knees.

"Try to listen calmly. It is hard to explain at best. And Anne—remember this always—knew nothing at any time. When I first saw you both it was together, staying in the same house. I never spoke to you apart. You called each other 'Sister.' I only learned your Christian name when you signed it in your first letter to me. I thought Anne indisputably the older. She seems so in her repose. You are very unlike, and she is a *violet*, Hester. I addressed my first letter to her as the supposed elder, and you as the actual elder received it.

I might have written to one as well as the other. You were both artists. There was nothing to undo the error, and it was to Anne that I believed myself writing in all those months. It was Anne I thought I loved and courted—you who replied. This is the miserable story. You know the whole." He paused, then went on with a difficulty that grew always greater. " Do you remember, it was Anne who came in to me first when I was waiting for you? Can't you fancy my bewilderment when I saw her standing there in the door-way, warding me off with her outstretched palms — remember, I thought she was my promised wife! I heard her say she had only come to welcome 'a new brother,' and it seemed to me the world turned round, and then she laughed in my face and ran away suddenly because she heard another door at the end of the room opening slowly. You know who came in that door, Hester. I saw your glorious violet eyes, your vivid face, your lovely dark hair, and you came towards me—if I could only see you coming so now— both hands held out, half shy, all gracious—"

With a swift motion Hester cowered down where she sat, hiding her face in her hands. "And you let me !" she cried—"you let me !"

Goodhue bent towards her, clasping her wrists

266

in his hands, speaking eagerly. "Hester, be just to me, now quickly, before you think of yourself. What could I do? If you suffer so in the thought that I played your lover for a few distracted days, try to think of what I saved you by refusing to play your husband. Think, too, of what I endured, loving the body of one woman, the soul of another. It was like acting out some horrible tragic farce. Day by day I had to see the body that I loved passing me, every graceful motion holding my gaze, and yet, when those dear, familiar lips moved to speak, they spoke a tongue I neither knew nor cared for. Could I have met Anne's soul alone, I knew I should never have recognized it. On the other side were your mind, your heart, your spirit, so familiar, so dear to me, but clothed in a strange body. Again and again, when you spoke to me of some lovely thoughts you had only written of before, I turned to you expecting to see the features I had called up so vividly when reading your written words, and then your unfamiliar face —can't you understand it?—would strike me as a blow. Hester, it is now the one face I care for, the one I was always seeing, always longing to see." He drew her hands from her face, and they lay so passively in his that his heart sank. "I have told you everything," he said, slowly. "I was almost mad when I let you see at last that there was some ugly knot. I let you cut it without telling you what it was. How could I tell you then? How could I tell myself what I felt? Have you nothing to say to me, Hester?"

She looked up at him with eyes from which the lustre had gone. "I can forgive you now," she said, wearily. "Of course, no one was to blame. It was an accident, that was all. There is nothing to forgive."

"I am asking more than forgiveness now," said Goodhue, slowly. He was speaking carefully, with well-controlled emotion. "Almost as soon as I left you, it came to me that, after all, it was you—your spirit—I had loved, not at all what I thought had clothed it, and then slowly your own beauty began to haunt me. Soon, too soon, I knew that the face I had seen as I read your letters, as I wrote to you, was never the face you could have worn. Your face, your eyes, yourself, began to fit your soul for me, and at last I knew you as you were, not as half another. Your own hands, your own eyes, the very way you sit as you listen, as you are sitting now, all grew clearer and clearer in my memory. It was not the soul only I wanted—

but you, all of you, body and soul, as I learned to mate them. Hester, it was accident that parted us, but to-day hasn't an accident flung us together again? I have told you everything. Now I dare ask more than forgiveness. I ask you for all that a man can ask, all that a woman can give."

Her hands were still in his, and she made no effort to release them, but he knew it was for no tenderer reason than pity as she looked up and answered: "There is nothing to forgive you, but there isn't anything left to give, either. As I told you, all that is over and burned out. There is nothing here now—can be nothing but cold ashes."

She loosed one hand as she spoke, and laid it on her breast. Goodhue caught the hand back to him, urging her by pressure and voice.

"Hester, try to see it differently. To-day, as I passed over the moor, I saw what you might have called a destroyed field of grass, burned out, nothing but cold ashes. Yet I knew because of that burning the verdure there will be doubled in the spring. We have both suffered cruelly, both been through the fire, can't we make that help us to a closer life?"

She moved restlessly, releasing both her hands. "No, the fire has been too fierce. It has destroyed. We can meet only for this hour in this world apart and on the terms we agreed upon. You are letting the earthly enter."

Goodhue's eyes turned to the causeway, forgotten in the nearer question. "Forgive me if I thought it the heavenly," he answered; "and my promise was that the earthly should not enter while we were in the world apart; you see we are not cut off now."

Hester's eyes followed his. The waters, receding as rapidly as they had risen, had uncovered the narrow, wet backbone of red-rock ridging across from the main-land, leaving a clear path to the shore.

"Do you mean that we are free to go?" she asked.

"We are no longer cut off, or, rather, you are cut off from nothing. For me—am I to live cut off from everything I care to live for, Hester? This is the last time I shall urge you. Dearest, you did love me — by that love so close, so womanly in the past, I entreat you! You can recall it ; trust me it can return richer, more ripe with promise than before."

He realized that she raised her eyes not to read his mind, but that he might read hers. When she spoke he knew already what the reply would be.

"That has all gone from me forever, not only for you, but for any one on earth. My hand offended me and I cut it off. My maiming is absolute and for life. That is all."

"You are deciding hastily."

"I am not deciding at all. Life has decided for me."

"Hester, see, I can gather your hands into mine, your eyes into mine. They belong there now as surely, as lovingly, as your soul was once gathered into my soul. You feel this. You are free to part them all forever, but can you?"

Hester shrank back, her hands, her eyes quivering from his hold.

"Oh, you only quicken me to suffer. I have decided. This must be the end."

She rose, turning from him to face the glowing western sky and the world between. A rim of the red, setting sun hung in the horizon for a moment, then dropped below the line. Down the coast the sunset cannon told the death of another day. A hush and gloom closed in with the falling echoes, and from the light-houses on the distant island leaped the blaze of two leopard-like eyes. Hester started when Goodhue's voice again broke the silence. He spoke lightly, she knew, to veil emotion.

"So be it. Come, Hester, inexorable angel of the flaming sword! The gateway to earth is wide open again. I have lived in Paradise an hour. If it has been that of a fool, never mind. Only—let me leave it without waiting!"

On the main-land two little half-beaten paths rose from the causeway to run inland—the one to the right, the other to the left. The right-hand path runs in and out between golden-rod and red-berried rose-trees, to be lost at times among the bay bushes that spread their heavy green leaves and gray aromatic berries above a yellow carpet of scented grass. The path to the left leads straight and uncompromisingly along the rocky coast. Goodhue glanced from one path to the other, as he helped Hester over the last stepping-stones, and they stood together on the main-land.

"There is your path," he said, "to the right, over the moors. That rocky way to the left, the steep, single path, is mine."

Hester looked up towards the crags of the right-hand path. "Mine is single also," she said, quickly. But Goodhue did not respond.

"Why do you make me seem so harsh?" she cried, suddenly, turning to him. "There has been too much suffering on both sides. At least we may think kindly of each other."

She held out her hand as she spoke, as if offering a friendly parting. Goodhue took her hand in his, holding it gently, as he replied, smiling:

"There was once a queen whose starving people cried to her for bread, and she asked why they didn't eat 'little cakes.' She was as innocent as you, Hester — but none the less cruel." Again he saw that she hesitated, and he waited patiently until she spoke, tremulously:

"We must part in peace."

"Forgive me if I seemed rude to you just now. But as you say you can be nothing to me, be nothing, I beg of you. Let it all end here. Let me go my way at once and you yours."

He saw her eyes turn from one path to the other, then out over the sea where the two great leopard eyes stared blazing through the gathering darkness. Goodhue drew back a step, loosening his grasp on her hand, which she had left in his.

"Wait!" she cried, quickly. "Oh, wait a moment. If to part like this is so hard, then I must be able to think of something that will soften it."

"I will wait," he answered, "but you will think of nothing, as it cannot be all."

Again he watched her eyes turning to the diverging paths, following the narrow way of each so far as sight might carry her. When she at last looked up at him again he could no longer read her thoughts. Yet her altering face seemed to him as a book, fluttering open in his hand.

"If you will not take my peace," she began, "nor my kindness, then you will have to take my confusion. We have been talking as if we were soul to soul. I am still trying to speak so. My feet seem somehow to refuse my path, and yet — they refuse yours equally. I am standing here utterly unhappy either way I look."

The salt airs blowing in from the ocean seemed wrapping the gloom about them, the odors of the bay-leaves crushed beneath their feet rose in aromatic sweetness. Goodhue bent over the hand he held, pressing it to his lips, then laid it gently in his arm and turned towards the path on the moors.

"Come," he said, "I am very patient, Hester. Let me take your path for a while. Dear, I accept your kindness and your peace alone for the present, for so long as you shall wish, and for the future—"

ImTheStory.com

CPSIA information can be obtained at www.ICGtesting.com
Printed in the USA
BVOW001558310313

316927BV00009B/134/P

9 781290 366502